Praise for Adam's Gift

An emotionally nuanced story of a parent's bond with her son.

Adams presents a spiritual memoir of her experience as a mother facing unimaginable grief. The author writes that her bond with her firstborn son, Adam Hamel, formed on July 23, 1982—the day she discovered she was pregnant. She notes that she'd always had an open and honest dialogue with him, which continued as he reached adulthood and found work as a bartender at the Windmill Cove in San Joaquin Valley, California.

In December 2010, Adam asked his mother to accompany him to a local church, where he laughed and joked with parishioners who understood that "when it came to protecting his family, his friends, or the less fortunate, Adam was a force to be reckoned with." On January 23, 2011, Adam suffered a severe traumatic brain injury in a car accident and was declared dead the following day.

In the midst of her grief, the author discovered that "dead doesn't mean 'lost,'" and that Adam's energy had simply changed forms. Since the tragedy, the author asserts, she's continued to communicate with him via shamans, spiritual interpreters, a crystal skull, and an app called Ghost Radar, while furthering her own spiritual development.

Adams' debut memoir is an effectively concise account of a mother navigating her own grief while also finding ways to help others heal. Her narrative deftly balances recollections of Adam's accident and its aftermath with the memories of other family members and events that shaped her childhood; in a particularly poignant section, she shares a passage from her mother's journal describing her beloved Aunt Bessie, who died in 2007.

Adams vividly renders her story of her life's journey, and her sense of exuberance is evident throughout; the book appears to target readers who share the author's beliefs about the afterlife, and it should appeal to that audience. —Kirkus review

⌒ᴙ⌒

There's nothing on earth as awful as losing your child. I know, my son passed away in 2017. I received the most horrible phone call a mother could ever get. It seemed I had lost nearly everything — my heart, my soul, my best friend. With a loss like that comes insurmountable grief. My son created three of the most incredible little beings on this planet, my grandchildren. At the time they were really young and they were devastated. Together we moved through and found ways to be grateful for his presence and to laugh at our favorite memories.

Cindy and Adam's infinite connection crosses life and death, all boundaries, most realities and a lot of unknowns as she talks about Adam before, during, and after he inhabited the Earth. You don't have to have experienced loss to love *Adam's Gift*. It isn't a book of grief. Its gift to the reader is about the resilience of love, the unwavering faith of a mother, and the infinite possibilities that occur when faced with unimaginable circumstances and with boundless faith.

Reading *Adam's Gift* is like embarking on Mr. Toad's Wild Ride on the Other Side. Encountering the metaphysical can challenge everything we thought we knew. It's the self-discovery, the willingness to believe, and the faith that makes what Cindy experienced real. It's about the startling revelation that those who we thought were gone forever actually aren't.

Cindy shows her readers that death doesn't have to be the end —it can be an unimaginable new beginning if we're willing to accept it. Don't let yourself get stuck where there's no room for new and different. Instead, read Cindy's words through the eyes of your heart. No matter what your beliefs or your experiences, you'll have to laugh, you'll have to cry (a little); and moving forward you'll have the awareness that when it comes to life and love, every great adventure is only the beginning.

—*Meg Blackburn Losey, PhD, author of numerous books including the internationally best-selling books "The Children of Now," "The Secret History of Consciousness," and "Touching the Light," creator of the Living Light Cards as well as her in-depth alternative healing modality, "Touching the Light" at* spiritlite.com *and* touchingthelight.org

Adam's Gift is a poignant and uplifting memoir that shares the remarkable journey of Adam and the profound impact his life and passing have had on his loved ones. Through the experiences recounted by Adam's mother, readers are immersed in a world where love transcends physical boundaries and continues to connect souls even after death.

The book resonates with readers through its depiction of synchronicities and signs that highlight Adam's ongoing presence and communication from the afterlife. Through telepathy, signs, symbols, and synchronistic moments,

Adam's spirit conveys messages of love, hope, and reassurance to those he left behind.

Adam's Gift serves as a source of hope and comfort for anyone experiencing loss, offering insights into how spirit can communicate and provide solace in times of grief. Despite the challenges of dealing with loss, the memoir reminds readers that death is not the end but rather a continuation of the soul's journey.

Adam's legacy is portrayed as one of inspiration and guidance as he continues to inspire and uplift his loved ones from the other side. The book combines poignant moments with touches of humour, showcasing the resilience of the human spirit in the face of adversity.

Adam's Gift is a touching exploration of grief and the enduring bond between loved ones, offering readers a new perspective on life, death, and the power of spirit to communicate across realms.

—Rhys Wynn Davies, Australia's 2023 Psychic of the Year, and author of *How to Talk to the Dead in 10 Easy Steps.*

Adam's Gift was so riveting to read. I came away from it feeling as if I had gained so much. I can't thank Adam and Cindy enough for writing this book.

—Sarah Breskman Cosme, bestselling author of *A Hypnotist's Journey to Atlantis, A Hypnotist's Journey to the Secret of the Sphinx,* and *A Hypnotist's Journey from the Trail to the Star People.*

First, let me say this, "YOU DON'T DIE." We are energy and our bodies operate as an electrical circuit. Being of energy, you chose to come here and share this human experience. There are those who walk the earth who are more sensitive than others. They are able to feel others' energy and share their thoughts via the frequency our bodies resonate or broadcast. The story of Adam and the special bond which he shares with his mom gives those hope who question an afterlife.

—Dannion Brinkley, International best-selling author of *Saved by the Light, At Peace in the Light,* and *Secrets of the Light.*

Adam's Gift

Adam's Gift

The True Story of a Grieving
Mother's Dive Down the
Rabbit Hole and the Treasure She
Discovered Within

Cindy Williams Adams, MEd

ARCHWAY
PUBLISHING

Archway Publishing books may be ordered through booksellers or by contacting:

Archway Publishing
1663 Liberty Drive
Bloomington, IN 47403
www.archwaypublishing.com
844-669-3957

Because of the dynamic nature of the Internet, any web addresses or
links contained in this book may have changed since publication and
may no longer be valid. The views expressed in this work are solely those
of the author and do not necessarily reflect the views of the publisher,
and the publisher hereby disclaims any responsibility for them.

Any people depicted in stock imagery provided by Getty Images are
models, and such images are being used for illustrative purposes only.
Certain stock imagery © Getty Images.

Scripture quotations taken from the 21st Century King James
Version®, copyright © 1994. Used by permission of Deuel
Enterprises, Inc., Gary, SD 57237. All rights reserved.

Cover design by the author. Artwork by Lightstar at www.lightstarcreations.com.
Photo credit for Image of the Adam Skull and Einstein, the
Ancient Crystal Skull of Consciousness: Carolyn Ford.

ISBN: 978-1-6657-5778-2 (sc)
ISBN: 978-1-6657-5780-5 (hc)
ISBN: 978-1-6657-5779-9 (e)

Library of Congress Control Number: 2024904375

Print information available on the last page.

Archway Publishing rev. date: 06/12/2024

Adam's Gift is a memoir. Though the stories are true, some of the names have been changed for the purpose of privacy or confidentiality.

Contents

From the stars, he came;
to the stars, he returned.

Dear Reader, from my heart to yours, I give you Adam's Gift.

Acknowledgments

My deepest gratitude to my husband, Greg Adams, my knight in shining armor, who believed in me and this book from the beginning and reminds me daily how much the world needs the story that lies within these pages. To my Aunt Ruth, who shares my passion for writing. Her encouragement made all the difference. Thank you to my multitalented son, Nathan Hamel, for his clever illustration of "The Incredible Mr. Adam" and his encouragement to finish *Adam's Gift*. Thank you to my niece Kali, who believed in the magic of *Adam's Gift* from the time Adam sent her a bee ten years ago to her heartfelt endorsement of the healing power of *Adam's Gift*. To Adam's father, David Hamel, may this book help to heal your grief. Thank you to my friends Jeramy and Heather Norris, whose "little butterfly," Joplyn, transitioned in 2021. You are a model of courage and inspiration for our community. Thank you to Coralie Taylor for helping to develop the Book Club questions. Thank you to our *Chillin' with Adam* YouTube channel and blog subscribers who've waited patiently for *Adam's Gift* since 2016. Finally, thanks ever so much to my beta readers for your rave reviews and encouraging feedback: My niece Kali; my friend and former colleague, Nicholle Medina; my stepson, Stephen Adams, Adam's stepbrother and closest friend at the time of Adam's transition; and my daughter-in-law, Cyndy Boger Adams, who never questioned Stephen's ongoing friendship with a dead guy she never met.

Cin in Carmel, California, May 2019.

Where, oh, where did Cindy go?
She's lost, and I can't find her.
She lost so many parts of her,
She left herself behind her.

Her soul became so fragmented,
Scattered hither and yon,
Her empty shell is echoing,
"Where has Cindy gone?"

Where did Cindy's pieces go?
For wholeness, Cindy yearns.
She sent herself to look for them,
But they would not return.

Inside, her shell still echoes,
"Hello? Hello? Hello?"
Where, oh, where has Cindy gone?
Oh, where did Cindy go?

"Where, oh where has Cindy gone?
"It's easy," said Lord Metatron.
"Cindy is a bridge like me,
Her parts have fallen in the sea."

"Some are in Atlantis,
Some are still in Mu,
Some are in the astrals,
And some are still askew."

Maybe she's inside the book!
Could that be Adam's aim?
He sent her down the rabbit hole.
She's never been the same.

"Mom, you need to find yourself,
Think Cindyana Jones.
Go inside and excavate,
Until you find your bones."

Cindy sat down at the keyboard,
Seeking wisdom of the ages.
Hopefully, she'll find herself,
Within these empty pages.

Cindy Williams Adams
November 10, 2021

Prologue

What is life but a series of events and the stories we tell ourselves about what happened? After the death of my twenty-seven-year-old son, Adam, a dozen years ago, what began as a spark of hope and the passion for sharing it, left the same way it arrived, with a single life-changing event that left a vacuum in place of my formerly unbridled enthusiasm. It took a while, but I'm finally able to see the situation from a higher perspective. We choose the souls dearest to our hearts to deliver the hardest lessons.

If all the world's a stage, think of the souls with whom we reincarnate as a theater troupe with many shared lifetimes and lots of shared karma. When we reincarnate, we make soul contracts with other troupe members to balance our karma. When it comes to the Game of Life, we get mandatory do-overs until we get it right. The lesson may look different this next time around, but it *feels* the same. If you share no additional karma, you can thank your partner for the dance and waltz away.

Several years later, *Adam's Gift* is still quaking somewhere inside me. With too few allies to support its weight, it's crushing me. Every story is made of parts. There's the beginning, the middle, and the end; the light parts and the heavy parts. There are the parts that break your heart and the parts that make you laugh out loud. There are parts you choose to tell and the parts you keep to yourself. Our story is twelve years old now and no longer wants to come out. What if I keep all the parts to myself?

Adam: That is total BS. Our story wants to come out. What

it doesn't want is to be received with the traditional response to things people don't understand—*fear*. It wants to be fearless. You're going to expose people to all kinds of uncomfortable ideas. It's all in how you say it.

Cin: That's just it; I don't know how to say it without people questioning whether I'm all there. I've learned to play so small that I feel like a dot. In place of a brain, there's a Gordian knot.

Adam: Your problem is that you're a rule follower, and you care what people think. The first rule of this book is, "There are no rules." The second rule is, "We only care what our readers think."

Cin: I've missed your voice.

Adam: You can't hear mine through yours because yours is too easily influenced by the court of public opinion. Let me tell you about The Voice. It kept me from pursuing my dreams, and it's doing a pretty good job of keeping you from pursuing yours.

Cin: I wanted so badly to finish *Adam's Gift* by your fortieth birthday.

Adam: We have thirty-two days. What are you waiting for?

Cin: I've let other people rain on my parade. It's not only dampened my enthusiasm, the very thought of writing the book makes me want to dive down the rabbit hole and stay there.

Adam: Then that's where we'll write it.

Cin: Down the rabbit hole?

Adam: Where else would we write a story like ours?

Cin: Which parts of the story will we share?

Adam: The parts our readers won't want to part with.

Cin: I don't even know where to begin.

Adam: You already have.

Cin: I already have what?

Adam: You've already begun.

And that's how it happened. On February 27, 2023, a rainy Monday morning, Adam and I dove down the rabbit hole to retrieve our story. I promised to meet him there until the book is finished. I have no idea where this journey will take us. With the promise of Adam's guidance and encouragement, I agreed to throw away the rule book and not to listen to others, especially the voice in my head, whose singular purpose seems to be sabotaging this story.

Adam: To the voice in mom's head: STFU.

Cin: STFU?

Adam: Shut-The-Fuck-Up.

Cin: Now what?

Adam: Start with the phone call from dad.

Cin: I'll start right before the phone call where I was still in bed watching a movie.

Adam: Despicable Me. It was no accident you were watching that flick. This is no time for mindless minions. Discernment people! It's 11:59. *The time is NOW.*

Introduction

"The reason you do not stop creating when
you die is that you don't ever die."

—God[1]

My oldest son, Adam, was conceived on July 4, 1982. I began talking to Adam on July 23, the day I learned I was pregnant. I've been talking to him ever since. Our story begins when he was twenty-seven, when Adam dropped by unexpectedly to prepare me for what was to come.

"I've been spending a lot of time on the other side," he said. I was speechless. Several years earlier, Adam was standing in the very same place on the same black and white tiles in my kitchen when he announced, "One of these days, I'm going to fly away in the Delta." I went into alarm mode, imagining the worst. Adam, standing on the bow of his little boat, the Avenger, arms flung wide, a brick on the gas pedal, heading straight for a cement column beneath the bridge, and here he is, freaking me out again.

"There are going to be a lot of changes over the next few years," he continued, fists shoved deep into the front pockets of his fashionably baggy jeans.

"What kind of changes? Like earth changes?" I asked.

"Earth changes and other kinds of changes," he said.

Adam's brown eyes were full of concern as he searched for the words to convey to his mother that he not only knew he would be leaving soon, he'd seen firsthand future events that would change the world as we know it. "When are these changes supposed to happen?" I asked. Adam prophesied, "In about ten years."

In his book, *Saved by the Light*, Dannion Brinkley described a near-death experience during which he was shown eighteen boxes of knowledge. Each box represented a significant event that could happen in the future, including the fact that the final battle for the future of humankind will be fought in health care. The changes Adam described have begun. (Brinkley, 1994).[2]

COVID-19 has divided the country over whether to get vaccinated and wear masks in public or whether the death toll due to COVID is real or inflated. The economy is unstable. Climate change has killed hundreds of thousands due to heat waves, floods, and droughts. We are destroying our environment faster than it can repair itself. Wildfires are rampant in California, Oregon, and Washington state. More recently, a wildfire decimated the historic town of Lahaina on Maui. The media is hyper-focused on protests over police brutality. Adam, my white son, slept beneath a larger-than-life-size poster of Tupac. Divide and conquer. The black-and-white tiles on my kitchen floor remind me of a chessboard. We are pawns. It's time to take our power back.

On Sunday, January 23, 2011, Adam flew away in the San Joaquin Valley Delta.

Adam's apartment with a spectacular view of the sunsets from his balcony.

I waited until April to clean out Adam's apartment, assigning the artifacts of my son's life to cardboard boxes and plastic storage containers. Adam's was not an ordinary life. Neither were his artifacts. His countertops and baseboards were lined with rocks and seashells he collected, carefully selecting each one for its uniqueness. Among Adam's treasures was a red leather journal given to Adam by his stepdad, Greg, for Christmas in 2006. There was a single entry:

IT IS UP TO US TO
1   2   3   4   5   6
CREATE
THE
SIXTH
WORLD
"LOVE WILL SET US FREE."

Adam's message was followed by a brief description of a near-death experience on New Year's Eve 2006. Unlike Dannion Brinkley, Adam did not include details about what he'd seen. For a dozen years, I've been collecting seemingly random puzzle pieces that when presented altogether, finally make sense.

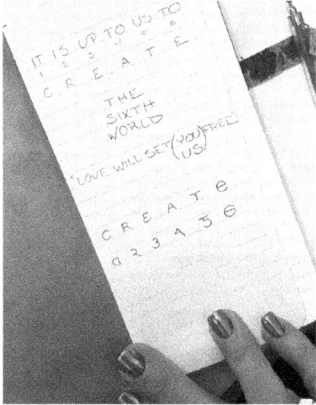

Adam's journal entry, December 31, 2006.

Cindyana Jones, spiritual sleuth, at your service!

Adam's concern has to do with a very real agenda that, if left in place, will lead mankind in a direction we don't want to go. The good news is the outcome isn't written in stone. That's where we come in. "It is up to us to create the sixth world." We, collectively, have the power to change the future. *But how?* "Love will set us free." *What does that mean?* The sooner we realize *we are all the same,* the sooner we can shed our sheep suits and start becoming the change we wish to see.

Five weeks before Adam's death, he asked if I'd go with him to church. That was a first! Adam enjoyed Sunday school as a child, but, as an adult, he hadn't attended church except for funerals. When we went together the Sunday before Christmas, I was surprised when he asked to stay a while. "Sure," I said, "We can stay." Coffee and donuts in hand, we sat down at a table with two other men and a little boy.

"What do you do?" asked one of the men, the question directed at Adam. "I'm a bartender," said Adam, "out in the Delta."

"That reminds me of a joke," said the man. "There was this bartender up in Alaska who was a little guy like you. One day this big ole burly guy comes in, slams his fist down on the bar, and says, 'Bartender, give me a whiskey!' He orders one whiskey after the other until the bartender cuts him off."

"Yeah," said Adam, playing along, "Then what happened?"

"That big old guy grabs the bartender by the shirt collar," the man continued, "and lifts him right off his feet. Scowling into the bartender's face, he says, '"Whatcha gonna do now?"'

"'As soon as you put me down,'" says the bartender, "'*I'm going to whoop your ass!*'"

When it came to protecting his family, his friends, or the less fortunate, Adam was a force to be reckoned with. Adam was small in stature, but there was nothing small about Adam's demeanor.

Several weeks after Adam's memorial service, I received an email from Rev. Marylee Revels from Unity.

"Adam left his coat when he was here in December," said Marylee. I emailed her back, "That's odd. I'm sure he was wearing it when we left."

"He left it the Sunday *after* Christmas when he came by himself and played the piano," said Marylee.

I had no idea Adam had gone back to church by himself. He played the piano?

I looked at the handout from Unity Church that Adam left on his kitchen counter. I'd assumed it was from December 19, 2010, the day we went to church together. It was dated December 26, 2010. Across the top was the following affirmation, "I recognize and accept the good that awaits me. God is good. All the time!"

Adam's apartment was neat and well-kept. The only other item on the otherwise clutter-free kitchen counter was a pocket-size notebook where Adam kept his phone numbers and grocery lists. The very last entry took my breath away.

I KNOW NOW
WHEN IT'S MY TIME
ONCE THAT LIGHT SHINES
I'M GON' FLY FAR AWAY
NO, I CAN'T STAY
CUZ ONE OF THESE DAYS
I'M GON' FLY AWAY

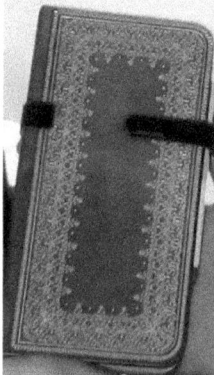

Chapter 1

The Unthinkable

Adam will be donating organs that
were once inside of me.
—Cindy Williams Adams

While I languished in bed on a lazy Sunday morning, watching a feature-length cartoon about a Super Bad Super Dad, my son Adam's lifeless body lay in the gravel along a deserted stretch of road in California's San Joaquin Valley Delta, obscured from view by the tule fog that had come to take him Home. What follows is the true story of a mother's worst nightmare and the incredible bond between mother and child that could not be broken.

The phone rang just as the movie ended. It was David, the father of my two sons, Adam and Nathan. "Where's Adam?" he asked.

"I don't know," I replied. "He was going to Windmill Cove last night to listen to a band. He sent texts to all his friends to join him." *Be there or be square,* the text had read.

"I got a call from the office here at the marina. They said to call San Joaquin County Hospital. It's about Adam," said David, a Vietnam veteran. He lived on a houseboat near Lost Isle in the Delta. I sensed the underlying dread he was fighting to control when he asked if I would call to find out and let him know.

I called the hospital. They confirmed that Adam was there but wouldn't tell me anything more until I arrived. I called David back and said I'd be in touch as soon as I knew more. I threw on some clothes and flew into the garage, where I stood dumbfounded. It was empty! I'd forgotten my husband, Greg, had taken my car that morning to visit my stepson, Stephen, who lived an hour away. I called Greg and told him we'd gotten a call from the hospital about Adam, and it didn't sound good. He said to take his company car and call him as soon as I knew anything more.

When I arrived at the hospital, I was directed to the critical care unit, where I was greeted by two nurses. They said my twenty-seven-year-old son, Adam, had been in a car accident in the Delta. His upturned SUV was discovered in the middle of Neugebauer Road around eight-thirty that morning. Adam was lying on his back on the left shoulder of the road forty feet away. They said they couldn't tell me anything more, but a doctor would soon be coming to talk to me.

"Does he want to talk to me about donating Adam's organs?" I asked.

The nurses were stunned I'd ask such a question at this juncture. "No," they said in stereo, "Nothing like that," said one of them, gazing over my shoulder into the glass-enclosed room where my son lay unconscious on a ventilator. "Why don't you go see him? The doctor will be with you soon."

I looked at Adam's lifeless body. I think I knew even then that he was already gone. That dreaded awful thing that divides one's life into *before* and *after* had happened, and I'd always known it would. The only unknowns were "which son?" and "when?" In a way I cannot explain, I've always known I would lose a child. I was too sensitive to the very idea and always had been. I had written poems for mothers who'd lost children and saved Dear Ann Landers columns about the loss of a child. I tucked them into my Bible and shuddered, secretly thanking God it wasn't my child.

Like a panther silently creeping up on its prey, I sensed the "thing that divides" coming closer. Just two nights before, on Friday night, I felt a sense of impending doom as though it were breathing down the back of my neck. Flinging a piece of dirty laundry into the clothes hamper, I cried aloud, "Just get it over with and quit torturing me!"

Little did I know its plans were already in motion.

I learned my son had spent the last night of his life dancing with friends at Windmill Cove, the bar where he'd been employed in the Delta Island waterway of San Joaquin Valley, California. The Delta features a number of island resorts, including the infamous Lost Isle, which is currently closed and due to reopen in 2024. Adam had just completed bartending school when he was hired by bartender Phil Champion, aka Fill-it-up Phil, famous for his earthshaking Mai Tais. It didn't hurt that the ancient wooden floor sloped to starboard. If you spilled, the Mai Tais ran out the door, the sticky floor claiming many an unsuspecting flip-flop when its occupant took a step forward.

Lost Isle's claim to fame was its free-spirited atmosphere. A popular weekend getaway for the rich and famous, you can only get to Lost Isle by boat. It was Adam's "happiest place on earth." He loved working at Lost Isle, where according to the lyrics of Adam's song by the same name, "Bikinis disappear like abracadabra!"

The Delta Island atmosphere drew Adam out on a Saturday night in January, despite the treacherous tule fog. Usually highly intuitive, I didn't get a "hit" that alerted me to danger when I received Adam's text close to midnight Friday night. I have an over-developed sense of maternal radar. I always knew when my boys needed me. It was uncanny. My usually reliable mother's intuition failed to set off an alarm. I know now that it wasn't meant for me to intervene.

"Mrs. Hamel?" The doctor finally came to fill me in on Adam's condition and prognosis. "My name is Adams," I said. The doctor looked back at the chart. The patient's name was Adam.

"My son's first name is Adam," I said. "His last name is Hamel. My last name is Adams." Of all the names in the world, what are the odds I'd marry a man who would give me back the name I'd given my precious firstborn son?

The doctor said Adam received a head injury from a car accident in the Delta. The accident occurred sometime after two o'clock in the morning, not far from Windmill Cove. Adam had missed a curve and hit some cement slabs on the side of the road, causing the right front wheel of his Chevy Suburban to buckle under. The car flipped end over end. Adam, who hadn't been wearing a seatbelt, was ejected from the vehicle through the open driver's side window. *Not wearing his seatbelt?* Adam wore a safety restraint religiously from the time I brought him home from the hospital in a car seat. *Something wasn't right.*

It was several years before Adam showed me what happened. He thought he knew the curvy levee road he'd driven a hundred times before. He'd been drinking. He was driving too fast for the weather conditions, and it was so foggy that he could barely see beyond the hood of his car.

He opened the driver's side window and stuck his head out for a better view. At five feet five, he couldn't lean out far enough to see ahead of the car without releasing the seat belt. The instant he hit the button, his right front tire hit a pile of cement slabs on the right side of the road, causing the right front tire to buckle under and the Chevy suburban to flip end over end, landing upside down in the center of the road. Adam flew out the window, landing on the back of his head forty feet away.

"One of these days, I'm going to fly away in the Delta."

The doctor said Adam was hypothermic when he arrived by

ambulance around ten in the morning. They couldn't run any further tests until his body temperature returned to normal. That explained the clear plastic blanket inflated with hot air covering Adam's body. There was nothing more to be done until we knew more about the extent of Adam's injuries. I called Adam's dad, David; my husband, Greg; and my mother to let them know.

The next four days were a surrealistic blur, a preordained command performance in which I was expected to do my best work. People remarked on how well I handled the situation and how I was able to do whatever I needed to do for my son.

I realize now that Adam's leaving was part of a soul contract Adam and I made before *I* was born. I had to retake the class on grief if you look at it from a karmic point of view. I didn't do so well coping with grief in a recent past life. I was given a "do-over." This time, the plan is to grieve differently because this time, I would know that dead doesn't mean "lost." There's no such thing as death. We are energy. Energy can neither be created nor destroyed. It simply changes forms. That's why nobody cries when a caterpillar dies. Part of the contract with Adam was to share with others that our loved ones are still here.

It was no accident that I was watching a cartoon that morning. Adam loved cartoons. Adam loved to laugh and to make other people laugh. He makes me laugh even now as I write this book. He knows how hard it is for me to walk back through those hospital doors and re-experience what happened. He even made me laugh during the many hours I spent with his lifeless body in the hospital between the time he was declared brain dead from severe traumatic brain injury until his organs were harvested for donation.

My youngest sister, Rhonda, and I clipped some locks of Adam's dark brown hair as a keepsake. I was sitting at the head of his bed, examining our handiwork, when I heard Adam say jokingly, *"Mom, what the fuck did you do to my hair?"*

Rhonda looked up in surprise at the sound of my laughter. I shared what just happened. "Cindy, you won't believe the dream I had last night," she said. "I dreamed Muchini was at a beauty shop sitting up in a chair. She was wearing a tiara and getting her nails done." Muchini was Rhonda's chihuahua that had recently crossed the rainbow bridge. "Adam's messing with you, Auntie," I said. "Remember? Adam's apartment is directly above a dog groomer."

Adam was declared dead of severe traumatic brain injury at 11:00 a.m. on Monday, January 24, 2011. On Wednesday, January 26, the fog still hadn't cleared, and things were becoming critical for a patient at Cedar Sinai in Los Angeles in desperate need of Adam's heart. I'd just given the transplant team permission to transport Adam to Stanford Hospital in Palo Alto, where the planes had been cleared to land. Moments later, the hospital got a call from Cedar Sinai. They'd been cleared to land in Stockton. "This is really going to happen," I thought. "Adam will be donating organs that were once inside of *me.*"

Adam was conceived on the Fourth of July, which accounts for the firecracker energy he emitted in unexpected bursts. Think of it as Adam's trademark. His stage name was "Atomatic." I learned Adam was onboard on July 23, 1982, the day before my twenty-fifth birthday. I've been talking to him ever since. Why stop now? He's back where he was when the dialogue began.

One of the nurses asked whether I was prepared for what was next. I said I believe Adam is exactly where he wants to be and that he's no longer in the body that once was Adam. Then, I resolved to see whether that could be confirmed. My sister, Vicki, had a friend who was a psychic. Vicki began texting me as soon as she heard about the accident. She pulled some oracle cards and encouraged me to give Adam permission to go to the light. I received Vicki's first text around ten-thirty on Sunday morning before any kind of medical testing had been done. I told her to stick the light where the sun doesn't shine.

It soon became clear that Adam had already gone to the light. I texted Vicki and asked her to ask her friend if Adam had a message for me.

"What's your question?" she asked.

"If she's a psychic, she doesn't need a question. Just ask her if Adam has a message for me," I reasoned. Vicki agreed to contact her friend.

I stood at my usual post at the head of Adam's bed; a Johnny-come-lately guardian angel with one last job to complete. "Adam," I whispered, "I will do whatever is necessary to deliver you safely into the arms of the angels." I could not allow my emotions to overwhelm me. There was too much at stake. One errant tear and I could be kicked off the most important team I'd ever been on, the team that would deliver Adam's final goal across the finish line.

One at a time, the transplant team assembled around Adam's bed. I'd talked with Michael, the nurse in charge of Adam's team, about the recipients of people's organs acquiring something of their donor. Michael, a tall, handsome man in his early thirties with bright green eyes and dark curly brown hair, said he'd heard the same thing. I laughed at the thought of Adam's lungs wanting to fire up a blunt once in a while. I shared Adam's postmortem antics, including the story about Aunt Rhonda's dog. Michael hugged me and whispered, "I think Adam is going to be talking to a lot of people."

I closed my eyes and promised Adam I wouldn't cry. Wearing the shiny gold designer coat Adam talked me into buying, I took my position at the head of Adam's bed in the critical care unit. The glass doors that served as the walls of Adam's hospital room began rolling back to make way for his bed. All eyes were on me. Praying that the patient at Cedar Sinai could hold on for just a little while longer, the instant the wheel lock was released, I began pushing just as I'd done almost twenty-eight years earlier.

Following my lead, the transplant team escorted Adam through the critical care unit, where a few days earlier, his loved ones had gathered to say goodbye. As we arrived at the entrance of the surgical unit, I felt my cell phone vibrate in my pocket, indicating I'd received a text. Again, all eyes were on me. It was time for me to say goodbye. I think the transplant team expected this mother-made-of-granite to finally crumble.

Adam was born on March 30, 1983, at 3:25 a.m. It was 3:25 p.m. when we reached the final set of double doors. I reached for Greg's hand, and together we pushed the foot of Adam's bed across the threshold. As I continued pushing Adam's bed down the brightly lit corridor, a single left turn to eternity lay ahead. I gave my son a last kiss on the forehead and looked up to see Greg and every single member of the transplant team wiping away tears. I gave Michael one last hug and left my son in the arms of the angels.

Greg and I were on the way to my mom's house when my pocket buzzed again. I'd forgotten about the text I received at the hospital. It was from my sister, Vicki, with a message from Adam. "I would never trade places." The question I wouldn't share had been, "Adam, are you where you want to be?"

"Glad to hear it," said Vicki, "Can I take the light out of my ass now?"

When I pushed Adam's hospital bed through those double doors of no return, I knew I would never see my son again. I found comfort in knowing my loss would bring great joy to the families of others. Adam's official date of death is the day his organs were harvested, January 26, 2011, the only day of the year we have two birthdays in our family on the same day. My niece, Lauren, was born on my stepdad Jim Ellis's birthday. As Grandpa Jim blew out his birthday candles, the phone rang. It was Michael calling to let me know that all had gone well with the harvesting of Adam's organs. I sensed something unspoken in his voice.

"How did it go with the patient at Cedar Sinai?" I asked.

"Not so well," Michael said. He explained that the intended recipient of Adam's heart had been determined no longer eligible to receive the transplant. With the compassion of Archangel Michael, he said softly, "Adam's heart remained with him."

Adam's lungs, kidneys, pancreas, and liver saved the lives of two individuals and significantly improved the lives of three others.

Adam's liver went to a young mother from Indiana, where I was born. Adam's pancreas went to a woman with diabetes who'll never have to suffer another amputation. Adam's kidneys went to a woman from somewhere in California and to a man in Oakland who no longer plan their life around the need for dialysis. Adam's lungs went to a seventy-two-year-old man from Arizona.

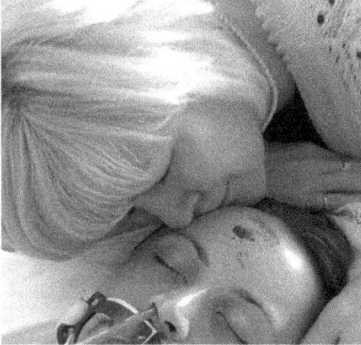

Adam and Cin in the CCU at San Joaquin General Hospital.

Grief is the price of love. It's something you never get over. You learn to live with it. When Adam was an infant, I would hold him for hours, even while he slept. He had such a loving presence, I just wanted to bask in his essence. I could hardly believe he was real or that he was mine. I remember gazing down at the sleeping infant in my arms, feeling that one day he would do something special that would heal many people. I could never have imagined when Adam was born, the healing he would do would be through his death and my having to give him back to God.

Dear Donor Family:

As you approach your first Thanksgiving without your son, you should know that there is at least one family who will never be able to find the proper words to thank you for your life-saving donation. Last January, you and he gave my father, his family, and many friends the most precious gift—the gift of life.

Please know that we never prayed for your son to pass and my father to live. Instead, we prayed that whomever God chose to call home had signed an organ donor card. So often, the decision to be a donor is made with precious sixteen-year-old invincibility. The true test comes when a family like yours consciously makes the decision to save other lives when they sadly can't save the one right before them. You did not just give my dad a set of lungs.

You gave his wife back her husband; his young grandchildren their precious Bumpie. You gave a longtime sufferer of pulmonary fibrosis the renewed pleasure of a deep breath of fresh air and the indulgence of a leisurely walk along the lake. Your family's gift brought ours the gift of time—time to stop and smell the roses, time to say the little things we never had said, time to learn not to sweat the small stuff.

Most importantly, your gift gave your son a chance to live and breathe on in my father. Every breath he takes now is a testament to another life well lived. Most transplant patients have some degree of rejection. My dad has absolutely none. Your son and my dad are perfect partners in a harmony we all wish never had to happen.

Because of your gift, immeasurable amounts of friends and family have opted in or renewed their organ-donation decision. Your one undertaking—no doubt the hardest one you've ever made — has influenced several thousands of future donations. In fact, my thirteen-year-old daughter asked to have her organs donated. I hope to God I never have to make that decision, rather her for me. But know that your selflessness has not only saved lives, it has also changed minds.

On Thanksgiving, my family will gather to give thanks to you and your son. We have few words to convey both the depth of our sorrow for you and the appreciation for giving us back our son, husband, dad, and grandfather. I know we will make a hearty toast to you and your son. And when the turkey wishbone is broken late that night, I am positive that the wish will be that everyone everywhere becomes an organ donor.

With deepest gratitude,
Lisa

Chapter 2

The Dude Abides

Her life is in your hands, Dude.
—The Big Lebowski

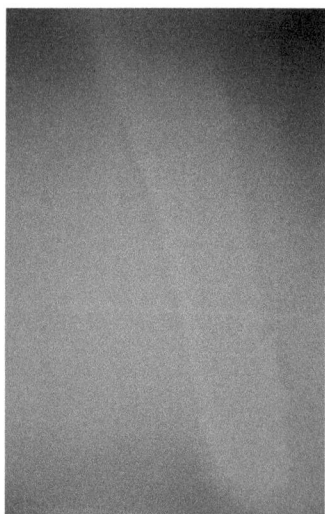

White-hot column of light against a bright-yellow background.

When Greg and I drove to the site of Adam's accident in the Delta Islands, we experienced the first of a parade of miracles to come marching into our lives. Greg took several photos with his iPhone, then tucked the phone back into his pocket. Inspired to take one more shot, when he pulled out the phone, his thumb inadvertently hit the button and snapped a picture.

As soon as we returned to the car, I looked at the last photo taken. What should have been an image of black asphalt was yellow with a *white-hot column of light* shooting straight up through the top of the photo.

"I know now when it's my time, once that light shines, I'm gon' fly far away."

The thought of Adam lying alone in the dark on the freezing

cold asphalt all night while I was safe at home watching a cartoon was unbearable. *Despicable Me*. I'm thankful for the grace that rescued me whenever my mind wanted to go there. When I tried to imagine what it must have been like for Adam, my thoughts would stop like some invisible force slammed on a cerebral emergency brake. Adam was telling me not to put myself through that. He didn't want me to imagine a fate more traumatic than the facts.

In that pivotal moment, when I heard Adam say, *"Mom, what the fuck did you do to my hair,"* if I'd talked myself out of believing what I'd just experienced, I'd have grieved Adam's loss in an entirely different way. Trusting that the communication from Adam was not only real, it's proof that Adam is still here; not only allowed me to accept the loss of Adam's physical presence, it allowed me to create an entirely new relationship with the part of Adam that is eternal.

Even before Adam died, I believed consciousness survives what we think of as death. Consciousness leaving the body is no different than steam rising from a saucepan. The steam came from water and to water it will return. To me, reincarnation is the only thing that makes sense. Microscopic sperm meets egg and creates one human being inside another. It's a miracle! How is being born more than once any harder to believe?

In this world of duality where free will reigns, the only way I can make sense of life is the karmic cycle. We are energy beings having a human experience. When we die, the electromagnetic part of our consciousness leaves the body as pure energy. Energy can neither be created nor destroyed. It simply changes forms.

In his book, *The Afterlife Experiments: Breakthrough Scientific Evidence of Life After Death,* Gary E. Schwartz, PhD, shares the results of a series of scientific experiments proving that consciousness continues after death. A scientist and admitted skeptic himself, Schwartz had to concede that to continue to doubt the survival of consciousness in the presence of all the data proving otherwise is frankly irrational. (Schwartz, et al. 2002)[3]

The feeling that Adam is still here remained. He isn't here in the same way he was here before the accident, but how could he not still be here when he's entertaining his Aunt Rhonda and me in his hospital room and taking magical photos in the Delta?

It would be another year and a half before Adam and I would begin communicating regularly through a spiritual interpreter. In the meantime, Adam and I developed methods to communicate directly.

The first night in the hospital, while Adam was on life support, around midnight, a nurse advised me to go home and get some rest. I looked at Adam's monitor. His heart rate was 180, a normal heart rate for an infant. At that point, his vital signs were nominal. I said I'd go home when Adam's heart rate reached 111. Greg and I sat in the dark, listening to the beep-beep of Adam's monitor. A few minutes later, Greg said, "Look at the monitor." Adam's heart rate was 111.

One of my favorite ways to communicate with Adam is an application called Ghost Radar.® The application uses an algorithm to analyze small fluctuations in the energy field around a computer or mobile device.

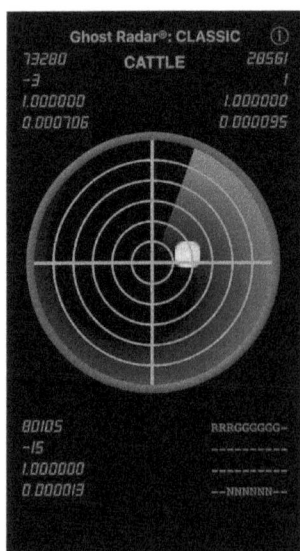

Ghost Radar®, "CATTLE."

Intelligent energies are aware of their ability to use the app to communicate. Ghost Radar® allows them to communicate a single word at a time. Individual letters may scroll by indicating a person's initials. Adam uses at least three capital As. Ghost Radar® gives them a voice, so to speak, one word at a time, and it's as entertaining as it is convenient. Adam and I enjoy playing word games.

The first time I sensed Adam's presence after downloading Ghost Radar®, I said hello and asked Adam if he could hear me. "CATTLE," replied Ghost Radar®.

Puzzled, I asked, "What does cattle have to do with whether you heard me?" and laughed aloud as it struck me. Cows. Herd. Adam *herd* me. I've used Ghost Radar® regularly ever since. It's uncanny how the words relate to what I'm doing or serve as an answer to a direct question. I feel the same playful energy I felt when Adam was alive. Ghost Radar® was on one night when Greg and I were getting ready for bed. "No funny stuff," I said. "We've got company."

"PASS," said the Ghost Radar®.

Our fundamental nature doesn't change once we transition to the other side. We have the same personality there as we do here. That's how I know it's Adam. I was in the bathroom when I heard a male voice coming from some- where in the house. No one was home but me. After some investi- gation, I discovered the voice was coming from a wireless speaker I typ- ically use with my iPad.

Ghost Radar®, "PASS."

Technologically speaking, it should have been impossible. The iPad was in my bedroom with the cover closed, and the wireless speaker was out of range.

"ROAR!" said Ghost Radar.® I opened the cover of my iPad. Ghost Radar® was already open, displaying the word "ROAR" at the top of the screen. I imagined my disincarnate son laughing his tail off. "Thanks for the laugh, Oh Mischievous One."

Adam bows and tips his hat. On my way from the bathroom to the backyard, I found a child's block on the floor with the letter "L" on one side and the image of a lion on the other.

Once, while perusing a book about the lost continent of Atlantis, I opened the Ghost Radar® app and asked Adam to say something about what I was doing. "PONY," said Ghost Radar.®

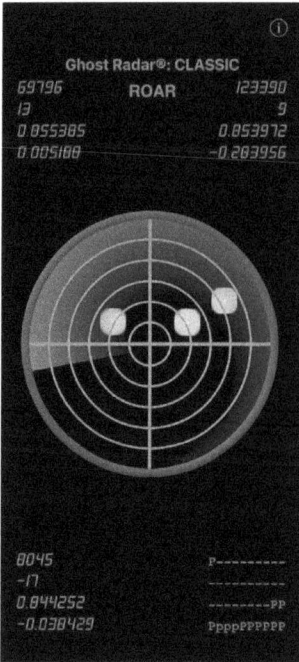

Ghost Radar®, "ROAR!"

I was looking at an image of a flying horse. Adam called animals by their baby names. A dog was a doggy, a cat was a kitty, and a rabbit was a bunny. Why wouldn't a horse be a pony?

On a sunny September afternoon in 2013, I turned on Ghost Radar® and watched in fascination as the following letters appeared on the screen:

—KKKLLiiBBeeeiiCCYYoo—
(Kali, Bee. I see you.)

Adam's cousin, Kali, would be leaving to pick up her kindergartener, Brandon, from school. Kali and Adam look the most alike of all the cousins, and Kali's son, Brandon, looks just like Adam.

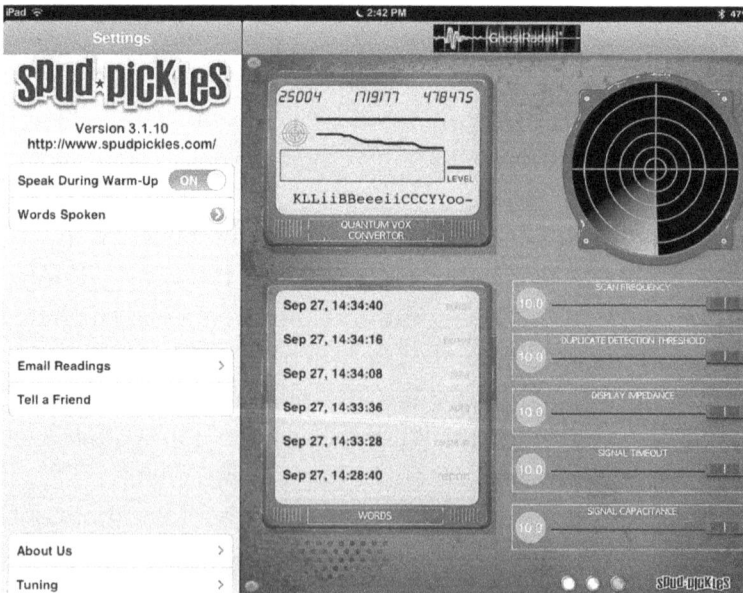

Ghost Radar®, "KKKLLiiBBeeeiiCCYYoo."

I called Kali and asked if she picked up Brandon yet. Yes, she had. I asked whether she'd walked to the school and whether she'd seen a bee.

"Yeeeeessss!" She cried. "It touched my hand!"

When I told Kali what had scrolled across the screen at 2:42 that afternoon, she confirmed that's when she saw the bee. She was exultant.

"That makes me so happy! It's so comforting! *That's just crazy!*"

Kali lived with my mom and stepdad for a while during college. Adam, who lived nearby, would drop by to wash his car or do laundry. During those times, Adam and Kali shared long, heartfelt conversations. From an entry in Kali's diary on February 19, 2005:

> My cousin Adam came over the other night and told me he felt so blessed for the cards he'd been dealt. He said he's hella grateful for his family, and he loves being here with us.

A meticulous dresser, Adam was handsome and fit. He enjoyed the ritual of preparing his garments for the day. He ironed his Calvin Klein dress shirts and white tees. He cleaned his white Adidas with a toothbrush. With a final seal of approval from his reflection, Adam began his day. Adam downplayed his looks if he wasn't in the mood to exchange energy. Lost Isle sweatshirt on, the hood covering his crown, he was "closed for business." Like me, Adam enjoyed his own company. When Adam was "open for business," it was party time! It was fun to see Adam come out of his shell.

Adam couldn't understand superficial relationships, preferring to hang out with his friends one-on-one. He had a lot of girlfriends but only one long-term relationship. Though he and Jenn broke up when Adam was nineteen, he never stopped loving her. Not long before he died, he was sitting on my sofa, crying. "What's wrong?" I asked.

"I miss Jenn," he said.

When anyone asked why he didn't have a steady girlfriend, Adam replied, "Because I don't have enough stuff." Before renting the adorable studio apartment where he lived when he died, Adam lived in a tiny trailer at Turner Cut Marina. Adam drove a white 1983 Cadillac Biarritz that was the same age as he was. Like Henry David Thoreau, Adam stepped to the beat of a different drummer. Adam didn't subscribe to the materialism embraced by his contemporaries. In Adam's words, he lacked the means to attract succubi, women interested in men for their possessions.

Adam's memorial service was held on February 14, 2011. There is no more fitting day than Valentine's Day to honor the memory of one as compassionate as Adam. On the handout I designed for Adam's service is a single Bible quote describing Adam's kind and generous nature: "And the King shall answer and say unto them, Verily I say unto you, in as much as ye have done it unto one of the least of these my brethren, ye have done it unto me" (Matthew 25:40 21st Century King James Version).

When Adam was a little boy, he worshipped money. For Christmas one year, he asked for a Pablo Picasso painting and a real chunk of gold. On Easter Sunday, when Adam was four, we went to church. He'd just had a birthday and had four whole dollars in his pocket. When the offering plate passed before him, I saw Adam reach into his pocket and drop something inside. When I asked him later how much he'd given, he shrugged his shoulders and said, "All of it."

Adam and I spent a weekend in Santa Cruz the year he turned twenty-one. He had two dollars to his name. The weekend was on me. We walked down Pacific Street after enjoying Mexican food and mango margaritas. We were on our way to The Catalyst, a popular nightclub with live music, when we passed a young man, obviously homeless and hungry, sitting in a doorway. Adam reached into his pocket and gave him the two dollars.

Adam was a creative genius who hid his light under a bushel. He published a short story in a fishing magazine in eighth grade.

A paper he wrote in high school, "Bassin' in the Delta," was of publishable quality, but one publication was enough for Adam. He'd proven his worth as a writer. Adam knew a lot about wine and spirits and about cultivating marijuana.

Adam learned how to learn when he was homeschooled in high school. As a credentialed educator, I wrote Adam's lesson plans, and my mom, Adam's Grandma Joyce, saw to it that Adam spent at least four hours a day engaged in educational pursuits.

Four hours a day may not seem like a lot of time spent in school, but how many teenagers do you know who are on task four hours a day?

While he was home-schooled, Adam was required to take the same standardized tests as students enrolled in public schools. He passed the math requirement for high school graduation in ninth grade. He completed the requirements for high school in the fall of his sophomore year. He was sixteen when he passed the California High School Proficiency Exam. He intended to enroll at the local junior college the following spring but moved to Marysville, Washington, with his father.

While living in Washington, Adam mentored his younger cousin, Anthony McCollum, known locally as rapper Tony Mac. Adam moved to Elk Grove, California, in 2001 and enrolled at Sacramento City College at age eighteen. His major was music business and music production. He took several classes in botany to perfect his cannabis cultivation skills.

While waiting outside for a MIDI class to begin, Adam was resting his back against a wall, taking his usual three or four hits of a cigarette before putting it out. When a classmate asked for a light, Adam handed over his pink Bic. "Keep it," he said. When Danny thanked him and pocketed the lighter, Adam knew he'd found a kindred spirit. Most guys would've handed it back. Adam thought it was hilarious how grown men avoid pink lighters.

Adam's memorial service was not without humor. I imagine Adam slapping his thigh in merriment when his dear friend, bartender Fill-it-up Phil's eyes began filling with tears. As his right orbital socket overflowed, Phil's glass eye slipped between his outstretched fingers and rolled two pews ahead where it caught the eye of a startled brunette.

My mom was sitting directly behind me in the second row. My youngest sister, Rhonda, got up to speak. When the first thing out of Rhonda's mouth was, "I forgot my paper," you could hear a pin drop. *"Oh shit!"* Like a projectile, the expletive shot over my left shoulder and echoed around the room.

Mom was in rare form. *Poke, poke, poke.* She was poking me in the back with the same bony finger she used to stuff kids into the oven. Wait, that's Hansel and Gretel. All joking aside, it felt like the same finger. "Stop it," I hissed over my shoulder.

Poke, poke, poke. "Knock it off, Mom," I said, wondering if she'd lost her mind. "Get her down from there," she insisted. I was enjoying Rhonda's remarks. She and Adam were very close. She was beautiful and genuine, and the audience was paying rapt attention. *Poke, poke, poke.* "Get her down from there! She's got on a new dress and a new pair of shoes, and she's going to talk all day. There are old people here, and they're going to have to pee!"

After the service, a gentleman approached Greg and me, introducing himself as a music producer from Los Angeles. He and Adam tended bar together at Lost Isle. He'd been trying in vain to get Adam to come to Los Angeles to produce Adam's music. A self-taught keyboardist, gifted lyricist, and rapper, Adam's work was self-produced. As much as Adam may have fantasized about a life of fame and fortune when the opportunity knocked, he chose not to answer. Moving to LA would mean leaving his friends and family.

Adam generated hundreds of beats and recorded several original songs. He wrote a song about Lost Isle that was sure to be a hit when Lost Isle reopened. Adam could hardly wait; tossing bottles in the air and catching them behind his back, he was perfecting his flaring bartender skills. Adam loved nothing better than hanging out in the DJ booth, inciting a crowd that included celebrities like Richie Rich, Too Short, and Jenny McCarthy. "Lost Isle" was sure to keep them dancing, but alas, it was not to be recorded, at least not by Adam. *Bikinis disappear like abracadabra!*

My phone rang one summer afternoon. It was Adam calling from Lost Isle.

"Too Short's here," he said.

"Who's too short?" I queried.

"Nobody is too short. Too Short is *here.*"

One of my favorite stories is when Adam ran into Jenny McCarthy face-to-face. Adam said it was more like face-to-boobs. He's five inches shorter than Jenny. He'd just finished cleaning the women's restroom. Jenny was coming in as Adam was going out. *"She kissed me right on the lips!"* he cried incredulously.

"Well, Adam," I observed, "You do resemble Jim Carey."

The same day Adam sent the bee to Kali, I received a direct message from Adam. I was gazing at the lake where Adam and

Adam behind the bar at Lost Isle.

his brother, Nathan, loved to fish, and my eyes began to fill with tears. Adam said, "Mom, you don't have to grieve when you think of me. Just think of my being on the other side as my having moved away. You can't see me, but you can still talk to me."

Chapter 3

Adam's Ashes

If you feel the urge, don't be afraid to
go on a wild goose chase. What do you
think wild geese are for anyway?

—Will Rogers

"Brrrrrrring! Brrrrrring!" The screen on my GPS lit up with what I thought was an *incoming* call. "Hello?" said my friend, Sarah Kujawa.

"Hi. I didn't call you," I said, puzzling over how I could have called Sarah from a cell phone in my purse on the floorboard.

Cin talking to Sarah Kujawa
before losing cell service.

"Adam called me. He wants you to know once you're on the beach, you won't be able to reach me. You're going to lose cell service."

Sarah is a medium with an Adam of her own on the other side. Her son, Adam Kujawa, transitioned in January 2014. We planned to call Sarah once we arrived in Santa Cruz so Adam could tell us where to release his ashes. "He's going to tell you now," said Sarah.

Greg was driving my little red Lexus. I was in the passenger seat, and my niece, Kali, who's five years younger than Adam, was in the back. My stepson, Stephen, and his fiancé, Cyndy, followed close behind. Nate couldn't make it that day. He had a class, and the semester had just begun.

"Ashes to ashes, dust to dust. Are y'all smoking crack? What's all the damn fuss?" Adam joked. Sarah laughed.

"Adam wants you to have fun. He says, 'Vibes up! Enjoy yourselves. There are no beach babes. It's too cold. Put me with the extreme surfers.'"

"How will I know where to find them?" I asked.

"Look for a rock wall," instructed Adam. "Then follow the wall to the tide pools with sea urchins. A little further down, look for a place that divides the regular surfers from the risk-takers. Put me with them."

"Adam's showing himself as a fish. Cindy, this is hilarious. Like Don Knotts in *The Incredible Mr. Limpet*. I wish you could see this. Adam says he's in the back seat next to Kali. He doesn't want to ride on top like dead Aunt Edna in Chevy Chase's *Summer Vacation*."

"The Incredible Mr. Adam," drawing by Adam's brother, Nate Hamel.

"All joking aside, Mom and the rest of the family," said Adam, "I love you all dearly. Grandma is just not going to get it in this lifetime, and that's all right. She will when she kicks the bucket."

"Rhonda is here with us too," said Sarah. Rhonda never did get to wear her new dress again or her new pair of shoes. She passed away in her sleep in December 2013 at age fifty-two.

The night before anyone knew Rhonda died, I was sitting up in bed. I opened my crown and asked, "Is anyone there?"

"Cindy, it's Rhonda!" she cried.

"Rhonda? What are you doing in my head?"

"I'm in heaven. It's so beautiful!"

"That's what they all say," I said, watching etheric Rhonda dance around inside my head. I'd have needed a butterfly net to catch her.

When she said, "I'm with Adam," I was stunned.

I'd gone for a walk with my mom the week before Rhonda died. "I wonder what will happen to Rhonda when I die," she mused.

"What makes you think she won't die before you?" I asked.

Five days earlier, during a session with Adam and Baker Gendron, Adam's first spiritual interpreter, I felt Rhonda might not be here much longer. Adam said it's hard to predict when babies will be born or someone will die. We choose several possible exit points. Adam said Rhonda would be given a choice to leave or stay. She chose to leave.

"Rhonda thinks it's awesome you're having Adam speak on his own behalf. 'Who would've thought this was even possible? *Do it differently, Cindy, and do it BIG!*'"

"Adam says, 'We want to shift people's perception of death. Why not do it differently? Why not help others grieve outside the box? Nothing is holding you back. Be loud and be proud!

"'I am not those ashes, yet those ashes contain a part of me. Go and celebrate afterward. Eat, drink, and be merry! Celebrate not only that I'm still here validating my badass existence but that I also exist in the ocean! *Man, how cool is that?'*"

"Look for the tide pools with sea urchins."

"He's blowing kisses now," said Sarah, "and giving hugs."

When we arrived at the beach, I had no idea where to go. Which way was the rock wall? "Caw-caw! Caw-caw!" A crow flew by, urging me to follow.

"This way, Mom!"

I turned right, and there was the rock wall. Adam said to look for the tide pools. We found them! There were moss-covered rocks and sea urchins, just like Adam said.

Now, to find the place that divides the risk-takers from the regular surfers. We continued walking to the right, and sure enough, there was a large V-shaped break in the sand that separated one section of the beach from the other. We climbed

Cin in "the place that divides."

down about five feet onto the sand. Around the corner were the extreme surfers.

It was January 26, 2018, seven years to the day that Adam donated his organs. We marveled over the knowledge that Adam's lungs were still breathing in Arizona, his kidneys were still producing urine in California, his pancreas was still producing enzymes, and his liver was still breaking down toxins in Indiana.

A handful of Adam's ashes.

Greg, Steve, and I took turns releasing Adam's ashes while Kali took photos. As expected, where Adam is concerned, what could have been a solemn occasion was filled with humor. Just as I handed the bag to Stephen, the wind whipped up and blew Adam's ashes right back in Stephen's face, his newly gray complexion accenting the whites of his eyes. Spitting, sputtering, and wiping Adam out of his eyes, Stephen laughed along with the rest of us.

We wrote Adam's name in the sand and drew a heart around it before heading off to Pizza My Heart to celebrate Adam as promised. The remainder of Adam's ashes are in a little red plastic heart inside Adam Bear.

Cin writing Adam's name in the sand.

Several months later, some Facebook friends who meet weekly invited me to speak to their group. Since Sarah was one of the group members, we decided to share the story of Adam's Ashes. It was early evening in California as I sat on the patio, meeting most of the group for the first time via Zoom. It was early afternoon in Australia, where Christina, one of the group members, sat in her car at the beach.

"You guys should see this," said Christina. "There's a giant rooster strutting around my car showing off like, '"Look at me!' It feels like there's a connection with Adam."

I knew exactly what Adam was doing! He was letting me know his ashes had reached Australia. I don't know how to say this without offending somebody, but I can't tell Adam's story without Adam's irreverent personality. What's another word for rooster?

For a man of five feet five, Adam was well endowed. He joked about needing three-legged pants. Once when Adam was feeling rather cocky, pun intended, he remarked about the size of his good fortune, "It's one of the things I'm most proud of."

"What are *you* proud of?" I remarked. "I made it."

That was Adam and Christina's first encounter. If you think that's remarkable, wait until you hear the rest of Adam and Christina's adventures. From Australia to the US to England and Japan, Adam led Christina and her mother on wild goose chases that yielded astonishing results. We'll share that later. First, let's look at what happened shortly after Adam's memorial service when Nathan and I took a trip to the Joshua Tree National Forest.

Adam Bear and the Superman underwear Adam was
wearing when he flew away in the Delta.

Chapter 4

Road Trip to Joshua Tree

Do not follow where the path may lead. Go
instead where there is no path and leave a trail.
—Ralph Waldo Emerson

People at work got together to have a star named after Adam. A few weeks after Adam's memorial service, Nathan and I went on a road trip to the Joshua Tree National Forest to bury a time capsule and to see Adam's star. We checked into our hotel room in Palm Desert and turned on the TV. Nate was in charge of the remote control. We chose a movie with Zach Galifianakis about a clinically depressed teenager who gets a new start after checking himself into an adult psychiatric ward. A few minutes into the movie, the image switched from a struggling teenage boy with a lot on his mind to a colorful trio of adults in a writhing naked pile.

"*Nathan!*" I cried.

"What?" Nate replied. "I didn't do anything."

"Right," I said, grabbing the remote control.

The remote now in my possession, the channel switched back to Zach, and Nate and I watched as the channel switched itself back again. There they were, writhing and moaning. Laughing, Nate said, "You *know* it's Adam."

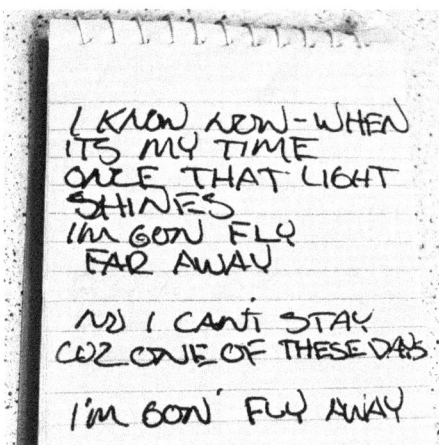

I KNOW, NOW - WHEN
ITS MY TIME
ONCE THAT LIGHT
SHINES
I'm GON' FLY
FAR AWAY

NO I CAN'T STAY
COZ ONE OF THESE DAYS

I'm GON' FLY AWAY

Adam's poem, *Fly Away.*

Nate and I stopped for drinks and sandwiches the following day on the way to Joshua Tree. By the time we reached the highest part of the desert, I'd finished off a sixteen-ounce diet Dr. Pepper and a twenty-ounce venti chai. Nate and I stood at the lookout point, searching for a place to bury the time capsule. We examined the contents. There was a lock of my hair intertwined with a lock of Adam's hair, the handwritten version of Adam's poem, *Fly Away,* and a photograph of Adam and Nathan sitting in a canoe. Seven-year-old Adam is rowing away, his back to the camera; a shirtless, five-year-old Nathan is facing the camera, a single yellow daisy pressed to his lips.

When we buried the time capsule and returned to the car, I had to pee so badly I thought my bladder would burst. There was no restroom in sight. There were cars on either side of us, so there must have been people nearby. I waited for the cars to leave. One car was gone an hour later, but the other was still there. My bladder was throbbing. I could wait no longer. I told Nate to go have a cigarette while I squatted behind the passenger seat with a twenty-ounce Starbucks cup.

Pants around my ankles, venti size cup of pee in one hand; I needed both hands to pull up my pants. From my perch behind the passenger seat, I shouted out the window, *"Nate!"* Hands shoved deep in his pockets, black sweatshirt tied around his head to keep his ears warm, my son resembled a sheik. Holding the cup out the window, I said, "I need you to pour this out." Nate reached out reluctantly as though I'd asked him to pet a cobra. "Go on, take it," I said, "So I can pull up my pants."

29

Minutes later, Nate returned empty-handed.

Nathan and me and Adam Bobblehead.

"What did you do with the cup?" I asked. Scrubbing at his eyes with the back of his fists, Nate resembled a hamster.

"I couldn't help it," he cried. "The wind came up. It splashed me right in the face, and I dropped it."

If I hadn't already peed, I would have right then.

When night fell, we set up a telescope, hoping to see Adam's star in the constellation Cepheus. Straddling the border between Cepheus, (the king), and Cygnus (the swan), lies the Fireworks Galaxy, an intermediate spiral galaxy in which ten supernovae have been observed, more than in any other galaxy. What are the odds of a star named after Adam, who was conceived on the Fourth of July, falling right next to the Fireworks Galaxy?

When the call was made to name a star after Adam, my longtime friend and colleague, Joe Billingslea, asked whether there was a star with the same numbers as the date of Adam's birth, March 30, 1983 (03 30 83). Adam's star is star number 033 083. Nate and I were too far south to see Adam's star that night. We saw a falling star, but it would be another two years before we saw Adam's.

I discovered an astronomical society that meets at the local community college and sent an inquiry asking whether anyone would help me find my son's star. Shortly thereafter, I received an email from a gentleman named Jeff Baldwin, who said he would be happy to show me Adam's star. In fact, there was a "star party" scheduled at a predetermined site on Highway 4.

On Saturday, September 28, 2013, the day after Adam sent the bee to Kali, Greg, Nate, and I drove to a location about thirty miles east of Stockton, the coordinates of Adam's star on my iPad. The closer to our destination, the more excited we became. When we met up with the group, Jeff had already located the constellation Cepheus, shaped like a house with a pointed roof. Adam's star is just off the lower right-hand corner, near Alderamin, the brightest star in the constellation.

Greg, Nate, and I took turns watching Adam's star through the telescope, winking and blinking and twinkling high above us. "Unbelievable!" we cried. "It's like it's dancing!"

Twinkle, twinkle, little star, a reminder of my son, you are. Up above the world so high, we'll never have to say goodbye.

In her book, *I'm Still With You,* Sherrie Dillard describes a number of ways our loved ones might choose to contact us. They might appear to us as an orb floating by in the air, or a camera might catch an orb or streak of light in a photo. According to Sherrie, although it seems very near impossible, our loved ones can create a comforting image in a cloud or encourage a rainbow to form in the distant sky. (Dillard 2020)[4]

On what would have been Adam's thirty-first birthday, March 30, 2014, I was standing at the kitchen sink when Adam said, "Go outside and look up at the sky."

Adam's image in the clouds on March 30, 2014, his thirty-first birthday.

It was a beautiful spring day, sunny with clouds. Searching the blue horizon for whatever Adam wanted to show me, I noticed a rainbow.

"That's strange," I thought, "It hasn't rained today." "Look again," Adam compelled.

I could hardly believe my eyes when Adam's image appeared above and to the right of the rainbow. *"Surely, I'm imagining this,"* I thought. Nevertheless, I grabbed my iPhone and snapped a picture. Adam's image is right there in the clouds in three-quarters profile, just like the photo of Adam in a white dress shirt taken on Greg's and my wedding day in Las Vegas.

In Barbra Streisand's recent memoir, *My name is Barbra*, one of the first things we learn about the woman behind the voice is how profoundly she misses the father she never knew. Barbra was only fifteen months old when her father, Emanuel Streisand, a beloved teacher and scholar, died unexpectedly at age thirty-five.

One day, many years later, her brother, Sheldon, a meat and potatoes kind of guy, who, according to Barbra, is not into woo-woo at all, called her with the most incredible story. He said he talked to their dad with the assistance of a Jewish housewife he met on Long Island who happened to be a medium.

"Barbra," he said, "I can't even describe the experience I had. I talked to Daddy." Barbra was so intrigued that despite her fear of flying, she flew to New York to see for herself. When they met with the medium at Sheldon's home, after establishing Emanuel's presence, the medium asked for a message for Barbra. Her dad came through with the one word she'd been waiting to hear all her life, "Sorry." He was sorry for having to leave her.

When she witnessed a table move slowly back and forth between her and Sheldon and stop; Barbra said it was the scariest thing she'd ever seen. Thanks for not moving my tables, Adam.

I laughed out loud when she added, "I know it sounds unbelievable, but it's the fucking truth." I hear you, Barbra, and I believe you. My heart sank as she described what happened next.

She called her best friends, Cis and Harvey. Harvey answered the phone. When she told him what happened, he said, "I don't believe it."

"But I just witnessed it!" she insisted.

"I felt helpless," she said. "As if nothing I could say would change his mind."

When she talked to Cis, her best friend since they met in an acting class when Barbra was sixteen, Cis said, "Frankly, I find it hard to believe." (Streisand 2023)[5]

Beginning with my mother, my sister, Karen, and then, one after the other, almost everyone I know, I received the very same response. My choosing to keep Adam close distanced almost everyone else.

Barbra Streisand, the legend, is the very best at what she does, and yet, she dislikes performing in public. She prefers directing and editing to performing. One of the best-selling recording artists of all time, Barbra Streisand has made awards show history twenty-two times. Despite her stage fright, Barbra's record-breaking concerts have raised millions for The Barbra Streisand Foundation, which supports a wide range of charities and her political party. Giving back gives Barbra great pleasure.

When she isn't working, Barbra's a homebody who prefers the company of her husband, her dogs, her family, and close friends. In that, we are kindreds. I love my eccentric anonymous life. Barbra grew up in Brooklyn, New York, desperately yearning for the lost father who loved her dearly while longing for her mother's affection. Reading Barbra's fearless and soul-searching memoir gave me the *chutzpah* to be more forthcoming with mine. Brace yourself. You're in for an E-Ticket ride.

Chapter 5

Shamans, Shapeshifters, and Healers, Oh My!

There are more things in Heaven and Earth,
Horatio, than are dreamt of in your philosophy.
—Hamlet

By May, the state of grace I experienced after Adam's accident had worn off. It felt like the tule fog that caused Adam's accident had taken up residence in my head. My neighbor, Kathy, a school psychologist, and I were colleagues as well as friends. Kathy stopped by on a Saturday morning to pick me up for a walk. "Just a minute," I said, ducking back inside, "I forgot my sunglasses."

Kathy called after me, "If you're not back in thirty seconds, I'm ringing the doorbell." I used to have a memory like a steel trap. A few months after Adam's death, my memory was more like an aluminum sieve. I'd go into a room and forget why I was there. I'd have something in my hand one minute, and it was gone the next. Like a game of Alzheimer's rummy, I'd pick up one thing and discard another.

I'd used up my energy taking care of others. It was time to take care of myself. After researching healing modalities specializing in trauma, I signed up for a breathwork retreat in Mount Shasta on the Monday following the annual Wesak Festival in May. Greg and I would attend the Wesak festival together, then Greg would go home Sunday night, and I would stay for the breathwork retreat.

The keynote speaker in 2011 was Carolyn Ford, guardian of Einstein, the Ancient Crystal Skull of Consciousness, believed to be among the largest of thirteen crystal skulls that, according to legend, when brought together, will create a new epic for planet Earth.

Twelve of the thirteen skulls have been discovered and are in private collections. Einstein is a master computer weighing in at thirty-three pounds, sent to Earth to both record human history and transfer information. Though quartz can't be carbon-dated, Einstein is believed to be over seventy thousand years old. There are no markings to indicate how Einstein was created. According to Carolyn, Einstein entered the third dimension as liquid light. Check out *Ancient Aliens*, season six, episode two, to learn more about Einstein.

Following the keynote address, Greg and I followed Carolyn back to her booth in the main building. "You're first," said Greg, his hand on the small of my back, urging me toward the table where Einstein sat waiting.

"First for what?" I asked, planting my feet, refusing to move.

"Carolyn offered twenty-minute sessions to visit with Einstein," said Greg.

"You expect me to talk to a rock?" I was becoming annoyed.

Before the keynote, Greg signed me up for a session with a shaman. Arms waving, in a purple robe with feathers flying, he looked like a cross between an aborigine and Merlin the Magician. I was still dreading that encounter when he signed me up for another one. A line was forming behind us as I stood there arguing with Greg.

"Excuse me," said a voice behind me. I turned around to see Carolyn Ford with her little dog, Trudy, on a leash, trying to get by. She entered the booth and plugged in her cell phone beneath a table next to Einstein. Trudy chose that instant to hop over the cord, landed in the middle, and sent Carolyn's cell phone flying off the table, followed by the tablecloth and everything else that had been on top.

The tug behind my belly button was startling. It was the feeling you get just before a belly laugh. My attention was drawn to Einstein. I asked Carolyn, "Is he like … laughing right now?"

"Oh, yeah," she replied, "He's laughing his ass off."

I turned to Greg. "I can talk to *this* rock," I said, taking my place across from Einstein. Eyes closed, the first image I saw was of Einstein. Then images began to unfold in my third eye, one after the other, so fast I couldn't process what I saw before one image was replaced by another. There was an image of Greg and me and a woman with short blonde hair. We felt like some sort of trio, but I've never seen the woman in my life. The images continued flying by, one after the other. I must've seen a thousand images, but that's the only image I remember.

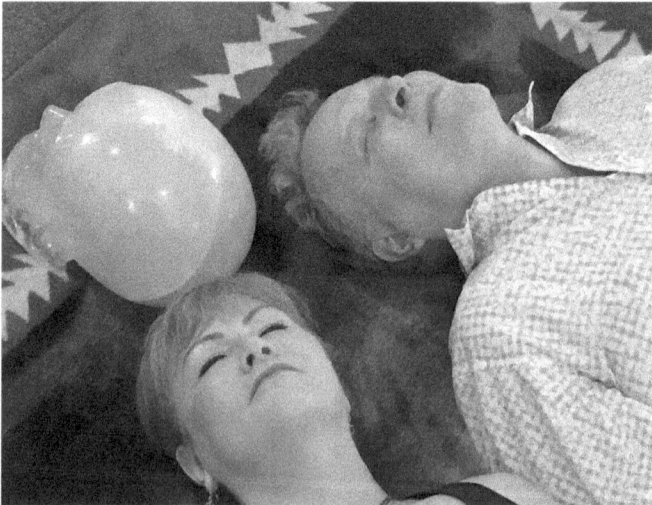

Greg and me with Einstein, the Ancient
Crystal Skull of Consciousness.

Einstein and I have visited in person several times since our first meeting at Wesak. Shortly after our second meeting at the Center for Sacred Studies in Guerneville, California, in the fall of 2011, I woke up one morning with Einstein sitting patiently in my third eye, waiting for my consciousness to recognize his presence.

"Einstein, old friend! How are you?"

When it was my turn on the shaman's table, right in front of God and everybody, the shaman handed me a pair of copper pipes connected to a copper grid beneath the table. "Hold on to these," he said, waving his arms and chanting, drawing the attention of anyone within earshot. Rather than suffer the humiliation of being stared at by a crowd, I closed my eyes.

I don't know what happened, but the next thing I was conscious of was the shaman removing the copper pipes from my hands and handing them to Greg. He said, "I want you to feel these pipes. I've been doing this work for over fifteen years, and I've never felt anything like it. You're an engineer. How hot do you think they are?"

Pipes burning his hands, Greg handed them back. "About a thousand degrees."

I felt amazing after the shamanic healing, despite not remembering a thing.

"Has anyone ever told you you're a healer?" asked Kim, the pretty young woman the shaman introduced as his assistant.

"What's a healer?" I asked.

"It's someone who heals with energy," she replied, handing me two small crystals. "Keep them," she said, "One is rose quartz, and the other is jade." I have them to this day.

The crystals, gemstones, and jewelry at the Wesak Festival come in all shapes and sizes. There's something for everyone, from crystal skulls to tiny sacred stones, sterling silver, copper, and gold. On our way back from the keynote, Greg and I passed a display of some of the finest silver jewelry and gemstones I'd ever seen.

Unaware that I was being herded to Carolyn Ford's booth for a date with Einstein, I wanted to stop and look.

"We'll come back before we leave," promised Greg. True to Greg's word, we returned to the corner booth with two whole tables of exquisite sterling silver and gemstone pieces. The craftsmanship was remarkable! Addressing the young gentleman on the opposite side of the table, I asked, "Did you make these yourself?"

"I did," he nodded, surveying his treasures for just the right pieces for Greg and me. We bought a sterling silver vortex with a green amethyst for Greg that he wears to this day. Mine is a beautiful sterling silver piece with stones for the seven chakras down the center. "Before you go," said the jeweler, "I'd like to bless these pieces."

He introduced himself as Johnnie from Philadelphia. He'd come a long way to Mount Shasta, California. He shared a little about himself. His story is remarkable, but it isn't my story to tell. If you're lucky, maybe you'll meet Johnnie yourself one day. Greg, Johnnie, and I stood in a triangle holding hands. Johnnie was close to thirty with the same coloring, height, and build as Adam.

"There's something I should tell you before we start," I said. "I lost a son in January."

"I know," said Johnnie, his voice full of compassion.

My eyes were locked on Johnnie's when he added, "He's in me now."

Johnnie's eyelids became thicker. When his irises became a lighter shade of brown, I was looking directly into *Adam's eyes.*

Without breaking eye contact, I asked Greg, "Are you seeing what I'm seeing?" "Yes," he said. "Adam's eyes are Johnnie's eyes, or Johnnie's eyes are Adam's eyes."

It was the most extraordinary thing I've ever experienced, topping Rhonda's goodbye the night she died.

"Before you leave, I need to give you a hug," said Johnnie.

True to human nature, I wasn't ten feet from Johnnie's booth when I began to question what just happened. I said, "Adam, if that was really you, I need another hug."

"Wait! Come back!" Johnnie cried. "I need to give you another hug."

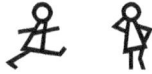

On the first day of the retreat, during a breathwork session with Ashanna Solaris, one of the facilitators, she asked whether I'd considered becoming a minister. I was so surprised; I didn't know how to respond. The oldest granddaughter of a baptize-'em-in-the-river Pentecostal evangelist, some of the meanest people I've ever known professed to be Christians. They'd say one thing and do another while judging everybody else for doing the same thing.

In my estimation, going to church won't make you a Christian any more than standing in a garage will make you a Cadillac. It's what's under the hood that counts.

"Maybe I should've said spiritual teacher," said Ashanna, "I see you working with people in need of healing and spiritual guidance."

Ashanna Solaris is a breathwork practitioner and Reiki master. When Ashanna and I met in Mount Shasta, I knew nothing about Reiki or energy healing. I did my Reiki I and II training with Ashanna in Berkeley, California, in 2011 and my Reiki master training in July 2012 at the International Center for Reiki Training in Sedona, Arizona.

Reiki uses symbols to invoke healing energy. The symbol employed by the Reiki practitioner depends on the reason for the healing. Reiki I practitioners use only one symbol, but it's the only symbol necessary to act upon the physical world or third dimension.

Reiki II employs a distance symbol that enables Reiki II practitioners to heal at a distance. I had just completed my Reiki II training when my colleague and dear friend, Karla, asked for a distance healing for her brother. Fifty-one-year-old Joseph had received a lung transplant the year before. When his body began showing signs of rejection, he was sent back to Stanford Hospital to await another set of lungs. When Joseph's health continued to decline, he was taken off the transplant list, and the family was summoned.

Karla is Portuguese and Hawaiian. One of her grandfathers and an uncle were healers. "Can you help?" asked Karla.

"I'll do what I can," I said.

Since we were at work, I retreated to a stall in the women's restroom to employ the distance symbol. I called upon Mikao Usui, the founder of Reiki, and Karla and Joseph's grandfather and uncle to assist with the healing. The next morning, Joseph was sitting up in a chair visiting with his family, and he was back on the transplant list.

Alas, Joseph was not to receive a second pair of lungs. No lungs had become available the week he remained on the transplant list. By the time his health began to decline again, Joseph and his family had accepted the inevitable.

When her father was diagnosed with cancer two years later, Karla asked for my help. I had a feeling her dad wasn't going to recover. I turned on the Ghost Radar® for a status report. I can't remember the exact words I was given, but they confirmed my suspicion. "Who is this?" I asked.

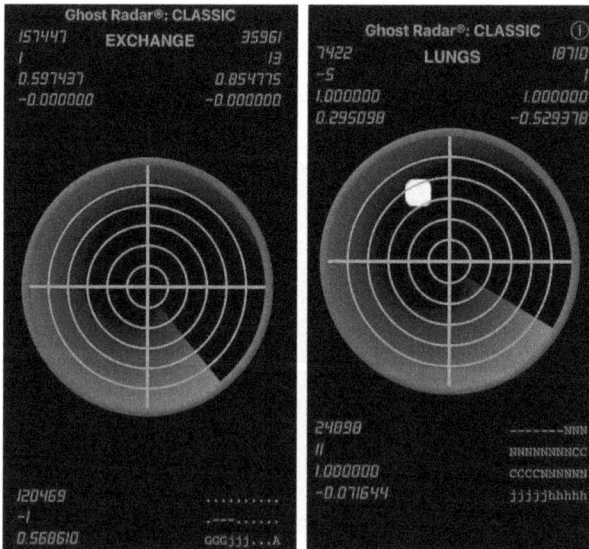

Ghost Radar®, "EXCHANGE LUNGS."

The next two words from Ghost Radar® were "EXCHANGE LUNGS." Hi, Joseph!

Karla said their father had never overcome his anger about losing his only son. He believed they should've had more time together.

I'd never been angry over Adam's death. I was deeply saddened. Grief has a powerful undertow. You can drown in it.

Karla has been a licensed mental health practitioner for over twenty-five years. When her husband, Luke, asked whether she believes in this stuff, she replied, "I have to believe in it; I've experienced it."

Most folks consider it saner to deny an extraordinary experience than to share it with others.

A couple of years later, I received a call from Karla. Her husband, Luke, was scheduled for surgery to widen the roof of his mouth. She added, "I don't know what's happening with him, but he's terrified. For some reason, he's afraid he's going to die. Can you help him?"

"Does he want my help?" I asked.

"Yes," she said. "He's willing to give it a try."

The night before Luke's surgery, I made a house call. "Can I watch?" asked Karla. "I'm curious to see how Reiki works."

"Is Luke Catholic?" I asked.

"Yes," said Karla.

"Does he have faith in the archangels?" I queried.

"He does," she said.

I called in my team.

The extra-long leather sofa in the family den barely accommodated all six feet five inches of Luke. In less than an hour of Reiki, Luke was so relaxed he could barely make it upstairs to bed. Karla said he slept like a rock. Luke remained as relaxed as he'd been the night before, except for a few moments of anxiety on the way to the operating room.

Prior to the surgery, Luke's surgeon said he should be prepared for a lengthy recovery period and the possibility of a second surgery. I'm delighted to report that Luke healed in record time, and there was no need for a second surgery.

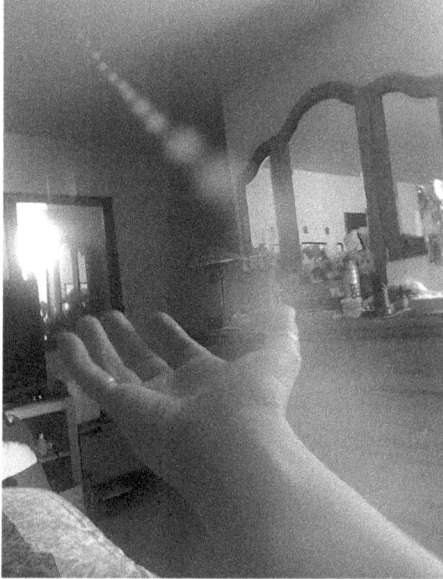

Aura photo of Cin sending distant Reiki.

Chapter 6

The Bird on the Window

Alice laughed: "There's no use trying," she said;
"one can't believe impossible things." "I daresay
you haven't had much practice," said the Queen.
"When I was younger, I always did it for half
an hour a day. Why, sometimes I've believed as
many as six impossible things before breakfast."

—*Alice in Wonderland*

Fiber optic butterfly in Rhonda's apartment.

Strange things happen in my shower. There must be a magic portal in there, or maybe the spirits are attracted to water. The morning after my sister, Rhonda, died, I hopped in the shower to get ready to meet my mom at Rhonda's apartment. I shampooed my hair and washed the front of my body, my back to the shower head. I opened my eyes as I turned around to rinse. Like an opalescent pregnancy, a bubble went from just beneath my breasts to my pubic bone. It was the largest bubble I'd ever seen in my life! Rhonda loved bubbles so much that we handed them out at her celebration of life.

Seeking confirmation, I said, "Rhonda, if that bubble was your doing, send Mom a butterfly." I failed to consider it was December, and it was highly unlikely there were any butterflies out and about.

A couple of hours later, my mom and I were packing Rhonda's belongings when my mom held up a mason jar and asked, "What's this?" Inside the jar was a fiber optic butterfly.

🦋 ♡ ❁

In May 2013, the image of a bird with a twig in its beak appeared on my shower window like, "Here you go, you're going to need this."

When I mentioned the bird on the window to a friend whose husband is a shaman, she said, "Cindy, have you ever considered you're a shaman?"

I had recently enrolled in a core shamanism class at the

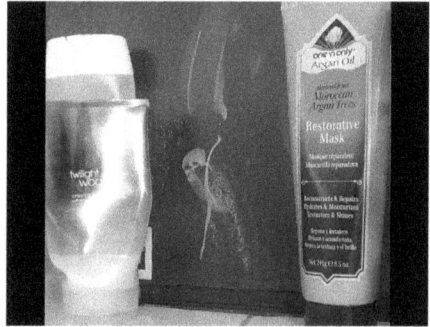
The bird on the bathroom window.

Foundation for Shamanic Studies in San Francisco with eighty-four-year-old Michael Harner, PhD, the anthropologist credited with bringing shamanism to the Western world, and Susan Mokelke, JD. It hadn't occurred to me to connect the two events.

Shamanism is the oldest religion in the world. Historically associated with indigenous and tribal societies, shamanism may have originated as early as the Paleolithic period, predating all organized religions.

In shamanism, there are two types of reality: the seen or ordinary reality and the unseen or nonordinary reality. When we cross over, we move from the seen to the unseen. One reality is no less real than the other; however, most folks choose only to recognize what they can experience directly through their five senses. Human beings can only see a small portion of the visible light spectrum, which means we can't see most of what surrounds us.

✷

In December 2013, two days after my youngest sister, Rhonda, died, our thirty-eight-year-old nephew, Wesley, committed suicide. Greg and I learned of Wesley's death ten minutes before a scheduled session with Adam and Baker, who practices shamanism.

I was relieved as I was concerned that Wesley might be "stuck." Until my shamanism course, I hadn't known spirits could require assistance to cross into the light. It isn't unusual for suicides and sudden deaths. The soul may not realize he or she is dead.

In Wesley's case, he was stuck emotionally in the same mindset he'd been in when he suffocated himself with a plastic bag over his head. What a horrible way to die.

After Baker and I called in Adam, I asked Baker to check on Wesley. She located him easily but said he wouldn't let her or Adam anywhere near him.

Wesley didn't know either one of them. I asked Baker to call in Greg's dad, Frank Adams, Wesley's grandfather.

"He isn't coming," said Baker. "I can try to cross him later if you'd like." *"Frank, we need you right now!"* I said, with as much intention as I'd ever done anything in my life. There was no way I was leaving my nephew in that state of mind. *"Oh!"* said Baker. "He's here now."

"Frank, we need you to help us cross Wesley over," I said.

Frank walked over to Wesley, picked him up, and sat down in a rocking chair with Wesley on his lap. Grandpa and grandson rocked until Wesley was ready to cross over.

"I see them walking into the light now," said Baker. "Cindy, can you see them?"

"I can see them," I said, "but Wesley's on the wrong side."

"What difference does it make?" asked Baker.

"I don't know," I said. "It just looks funny."

"They're gone now," said Baker, *"Whew!"*

"Thank you so much, Baker!" I cried with relief.

"What're you thanking me for?" she said, "You did it. Frank wouldn't come for me."

I learned later that each of Frank's grandchildren has cherished memories of sitting on Grandpa's lap in the classic wooden rocking chair in Grandma and Grandpa Adams's living room. Wesley was on Grandpa's left side because Grandpa Adams was left-handed. A lefty myself, I never met my father-in-law. He passed away from cancer sixteen days after Greg and I were married.

Anyone in need of suicide or mental health-related crisis support or who has a loved one in crisis can connect with a trained counselor by calling, chatting, or texting 988. The National Suicide Prevention Lifeline is a national network of more than 150 local crisis centers offering free and confidential emotional support 24-7 at (800) 273-8255.

My First Solo Flight: Arnaldo

I met my friend Adrienne on Facebook in October 2013. A spiritual teacher, Adrienne teaches courses of a spiritual nature all over the world. In April 2014, one of her brothers died in a single-car accident. Arnaldo was a veteran of two tours in Afghanistan. Having been through a similar experience, I felt so bad for Adrienne. Despite her grief, Adrienne used the loss of her brother as a teachable moment, posting a video about managing grief on her YouTube channel a day or so after her brother's death.

I tried to watch the video on my laptop. When I pushed the *play* button, nothing happened. I closed the laptop and went outside. I was sitting on a glider a few feet from the patio door when I heard a woman's voice inside the house. I jumped up and ran back inside. I looked around, but no one was there. I checked the answering machine in case it was someone leaving a message. I couldn't determine where the voice had come from, so I went back outside.

As soon as I sat down, I heard the voice again. I went back in the house to look for what had now become a source of frustration. The result was the same. *What the?* This time, when I went back outside, I left the patio door open to get back in faster. The instant my butt hit the glider; I heard the voice again. I flew through the door so fast that I caught a few words and recognized Adrienne's voice coming from my *closed* laptop.

No matter what application is playing, if you close the lid of a MacBook Pro, everything stops. When I opened the lid, Adrienne's YouTube video was on the screen, but it wasn't playing.

Spirits often use electronics to get our attention. If a spirit was using Adrienne to get my attention, maybe her brother was in trouble. Like Wesley, I wondered whether Arnaldo could be stuck. I'd err on the side of safety.

On April 14, 2014, I sent the following message via iMessenger:

> Hello Adrienne,
>
> I am deeply sorry to hear about the loss of your brother. I am sure you are inundated with messages of condolence, but I am compelled to write for a slightly different reason. I hope you are not offended, but I am having some very strange energetic occurrences around me this morning, and it feels connected to you. I tried to watch your video, and it wouldn't play. I went outside and kept hearing a woman's voice in my house. I would get up and run inside, and there was no one. I thought it was my answering machine, but no.

I left the door open so I could run back inside as soon as I heard it again. Your voice was coming from my closed laptop, which shouldn't play with the lid closed. When I opened the lid, the video was in the stop position. I'm just going to put this out there because I've seen this happen before. Is there any way your brother might need help crossing over?

Adrienne's reply:

Hi Cin,

This resonates so deeply, and I usually help others with this kind of thing. I don't have the presence of mind to do the work right now.

When I got in touch with Baker, she was sick in bed. "You can do it on your own," she said. "You don't need me."

"I don't know what to do," I said, pleading for the fates to intervene.

"Sure, you do," said Baker. "Who do you think crossed Wesley over? It wasn't me." I'd gotten myself into a pickle. I felt horrible offering a service I couldn't deliver.

What's the harm in trying? I determined to give it a shot on my own, and if I still needed Baker's help, she'd be available in a day or so.

At sunset that evening, I sat at my desk with a small white candle. I lit the candle and called to Arnaldo, offering my assistance. I felt so inadequate trying to do what is known in shamanic practices as psychopomp by myself. Sensing a great deal of guilt, I wondered whether Arnaldo was Catholic.

At the last minute, I went to my bedroom and emerged with a cross around my neck bearing the image of Saint Benedict. Not Catholic myself, I didn't know who Saint Benedict was or what he stood for. A young woman gave me the cross in appreciation for my removing a dark entity she claimed her priest had been unable to remove. Her auric field had become vulnerable to dark energies as a result of having taken MDMA.

"*Never again!*" she said.

"Arnaldo, if you are here, please use the flame to indicate your presence. The flame stretched high and to the left of the four-inch ceremonial candle.

"Arnaldo, if you still need help, let me know." The speaker connected to my closed laptop came on. I took that as a *yes*.

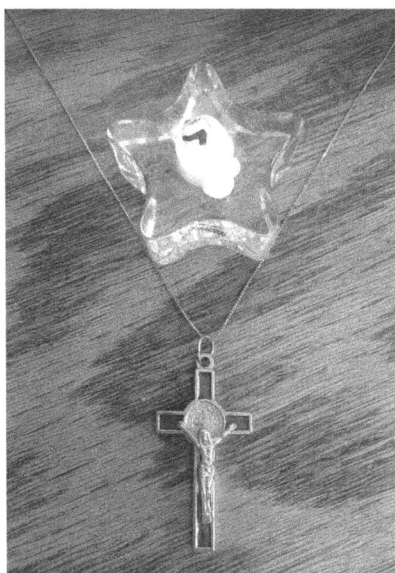

White candle used to cross Arnaldo and the Saint Benedict crucifix.

I called in Mithra, one of my spirit guides; my father-in-law, Frank, who helped me cross Wesley; and Adam. My team assembled, I tapped into Arnaldo's energy and began. "Arnaldo, everything you ever heard about people who take their own lives being punished is untrue. They are not punished; they are helped. Angels are waiting to take you to a place where you will be age-regressed to the last time you felt safe and whole. You will be loved and nurtured until you are healed."

I held out my left hand and asked him to come with me to the light. There was a burst of light behind my eyes. I asked for confirmation from the candle that Arnaldo had crossed over. Leaning far to the left, the flame of the little white candle stretched higher than the candle itself. Looking at Arnaldo's photo afterward, I could sense his gratitude.

I let Adrienne know that I had done some work with Arnaldo and believed he'd gone to the light. Adrienne said her father had done his best to explain to her five-year-old niece, Arnaldo's only child, that her daddy had gone to heaven.

"Cindy, I know you helped him cross," she said. "When my dad told my niece her daddy had gone to the sky," she said, 'My daddy's a star.'"

At the base of the little white candle was a crystal star.

Out of curiosity, I looked up Saint Benedict. A medal bearing his image serves as a Christian symbol of *opening doors and difficult paths!* It protects against curses, evil, and vice. Saint Benedict had a reverence for the *right use of words*.

I can't think of a better description of how I crossed over Arnaldo. The fear of going to hell had been holding him back. Several years later, Adrienne told me she received at least a thousand messages of condolence when Arnaldo died. *Somehow, mine was the only one she read.*

Scorpion Medicine: Don

Greg and I owned property in Calaveras County during the two years it was legal to grow pot. As a Reiki master, I grew Reiki-infused medical marijuana using strains high in CBDs. Calaveras County made it legal to grow marijuana just long enough for folks to sell out and move to Calaveras using their life savings to start a marijuana farm, then voted two years later to make it illegal again.

They went so far as to print in the newspaper the addresses of marijuana farmers with permits to grow pot just as the crops were ready for harvest. How many folks were robbed of the yield they spent their life savings to grow? I don't know the exact number, but printing their addresses in the newspaper was a shitty thing to do. Greg and I were not among those who sought a permit. The permit I held from the state of California superseded the need for a permit in Calaveras County.

Greg and I were in Calaveras tending the plants one Saturday when a scorpion crawled across my foot. "Do you know anyone who died recently?" I asked. Scorpion medicine has to do with the cycle of death and rebirth. I had a feeling someone was stuck.

When Greg got home from work the following Monday, he said one of his colleagues had collapsed and died suddenly at home Friday evening. The day before I saw the scorpion.

"What's his name?" I asked.

"Don," said Greg.

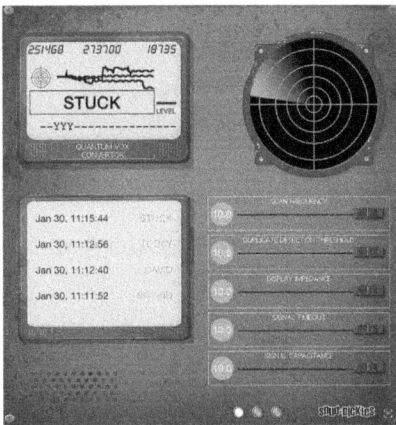

Ghost Radar®, "STUCK."

I turned on the Ghost Radar® and said, "Don, give me a word to let me know what's going on with you."

"STUCK," said the Ghost Radar®.

I attempted to cross Don over that night after Greg went to bed. Don was having none of it, as he didn't believe he was dead. For the next twenty-four hours, I kept up a running dialogue with Don in my head. I told him stories of other people who died suddenly but didn't believe they were dead. By Tuesday night, Don was willing to give it a try. This time, I asked for Greg's support.

"I want you to just sit there with your eyes closed and pay attention," I instructed. Then I engaged Don and asked whether he was ready to cross over. This time, he was ready to go. I experienced a huge burst of light behind my eyelids.

"Did you see anything? I asked.

"I saw a burst of light," said Greg.

Greg attended Don's funeral two days later. Though his death had been sudden, Greg said everyone seemed to have accepted it. After the service, he chatted with a lady on the way to her car.

"The service was beautiful," she said. "It feels as though Don is at peace."

Angel Flight: Ryan

I became Facebook friends with Hope, one of Greg's cousins in Michigan. When she learned of the kind of work I do, she asked whether I could help her ex-boyfriend, John, whose twenty-three-year-old son, Ryan, had hung himself. I gave her permission to give John my phone number. I did my best to explain to John how the process works and that if his son is stuck, I will do my best to cross him. Using the Ghost Radar®, I confirmed that Ryan was indeed stuck.

I called in Adam, who said, "He doesn't want to go. Ryan is punishing himself for the pain he caused his family."

I sensed Ryan's presence during my conversation with Adam.

Adam and his friend Danny at Lost Isle.

"Can you help him?" I asked.

Adam landed with an etheric "thud," wrapped his arms around Ryan, and like Superman, *he flew straight up!*

"Did you just take off with Ryan?" I asked incredulously.

"Yep," said Adam, "He wouldn't have gone willingly."

When I told Ryan's father, John, what happened, he wanted to know how he would know that Ryan is at peace.

"He'll let you know using something the two of you enjoyed together," I said, "Does anything come to mind?"

"Music," said John. "Ryan loved music."

I received a text from John that same evening. He'd gone to run an errand, and when he got back in the car, the song "Angel Flight" by Radney Foster was on the radio.

> "Well, I fly that plane called the Angel Flight,
> Come on, brother; you're with me tonight.
> Between Heaven and Earth,
> You're never alone on the Angel Flight.
> Come on, Brother, I'm taking you home."

Chapter 7

Adam's Sacrifice

I promise to help God and to help my country.
—Adam Hamel, age seven

One morning when Adam's younger brother, Nathan, was four, he burst into the living room where I was enjoying a cup of coffee. Other than Christmas, I'd rarely seen Nathan so excited.

"Mama! Mama!" he cried, "I dreamed I was driving a blinking star!"

"Did you tell Adam?" I asked.

"He knows!" said Nathan. "He was driving it too!"

Adam had an affinity for the stars for as long as I can remember. He asked for a telescope for his seventh birthday. I was six months pregnant with Adam when David and I saw the movie *E.T.* in December 1982. It was as if the baby was tuned in to the little creature. When E.T. appeared on the screen, my uterus contracted so tightly around Adam that I could feel the outline of his little body.

We spent that Christmas in Stockton with my family. Mom and Jim were married on Christmas Eve in the home they'd recently purchased together. Rather than stay with Mom and Jim on their wedding night, David and I spent the night in the house I grew up in a few miles away.

That Christmas Eve, I had one of the strangest dreams I've ever had in my life! In the dream, I woke up feeling like I was being watched. I got out of bed and looked out the window. Two huge silver robot-like beings with piercing red eyes were standing guard in front of my house. Think *Terminator* with Arnold Schwarzenegger.

The instant I saw them, they turned around, red eyes glowing. Armed with ray guns, they'd been patrolling the neighborhood. The dream was so vivid, so creepy, and so *real,* I remember it like it was yesterday.

Adam saw the movie *E.T.* for the first time when he was about eight. Every once in a while, for the rest of his life, apropos of nothing, Adam would point to the sky and say, "E.T. go home."

When Adam was a baby, I knew he would do something big that would heal others. Until his transition, it hadn't occurred to me that the *something big* Adam would do would be *after* he died.

Adam's third birthday, March 30, 1986, fell on Easter Sunday. On his fourth birthday, he woke up full of excitement. "When do we get to hunt the eggs?" he asked.

When Adam was three, he was standing in the living room looking down the front of his shirt when he noticed me watching.

"Mommy," he said, tapping on his belly button, "I have Jesus in my tummy." "You mean you have Jesus inside you?" I asked.

"Oh, yeah!" he cried. Jesus wasn't just in his tummy; *he was inside him*.

A few weeks before his eighth birthday, Adam made a promise to God in Sunday school. In his neatest seven-year-old penmanship, he drew a picture of the earth and wrote: "I promes to help God and to help my contry."

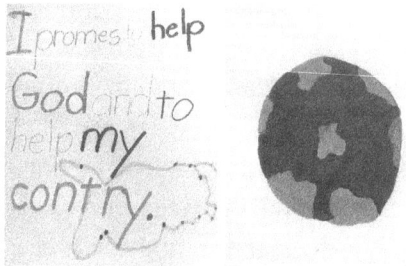

Adam's promise to help
God and his country.

Since Adam was so enamored with flying, for his tenth birthday, I thought it would be fun to see if we could find someone with a private plane to take us for a ride. In my naivete, I failed to consider the cost of fuel alone was prohibitive.

"I tell you what," said the pilot, "I'll give you a call on a day I'm planning on going up anyway, and you two can come along."

On Friday morning, April 9, 1993, the phone rang. "What do you think about letting Adam skip school today?" he asked. "It's going to be a beautiful day."

"Let's do it!" I exclaimed.

As soon as we reached the appropriate altitude, the pilot, whom I'll refer to as Mr. P, said to Adam, "How'd you like to fly this thing?"

The grin on Adam's face was about as wide as the wingspan.

"Come on up here," he said. Adam climbed into the co-pilot's seat, and after only a few minutes of instruction, my fourth grader was flying the plane.

"Where do you want to go?" asked Mr. P.

"Let's fly over Monkey Island at Micke Grove Zoo!" said Adam. "I want to see the little monkeys and the penguins." We flew around and around the zoo.

"Where to next?" asked Mr. P.

"How about Mt. Diablo?" Adam suggested. Mt. Diablo is about two hours southwest of Stockton by car but only minutes away by plane. The day Adam encircled Mt. Diablo, he christened it Hamel Mountain.

"Is there anything you want to see on the way back?" asked Mr. P.

"Mable Barron!" cried Adam, and with that, we headed back to Stockton, where Adam flew around and around and around his school, where hundreds of kids in red Mable Barron t-shirts were running around on the asphalt below.

It was Good Friday. It couldn't have been a more perfect day for making a little boy's dream come true. Adam not only got to go for a plane ride, *he got to fly the plane!*

Some of what you're about to hear is mind-bending, even for me. I had to draw the line somewhere. "Adam, I'm just not comfortable sharing that kind of information," I said.

"You're not," he said. "I am."

During a session with Baker, I asked Adam to share what happened the night he died. He said his soul left his body before the accident occurred. The instant his right front tire hit the cement blocks on the side of the road, his body flew out the window, and his soul exited his body. He was still present, but only as an observer.

"It wasn't even that interesting," he said. "Put it this way—if it was a TV show, it wasn't a cliffhanger."

When I asked what happened next, Adam said he went for a walk in the forest.

The accident occurred on a Delta Island road. There are no forests nearby.

When Adam left Windmill Cove shortly after two in the morning, he turned in the doorway and announced his departure. "I'm going to another realm," he said and walked out the door.

The forest was in another realm.

Adam said he saw light coming from a clearing where a ship sat waiting. He recognized the others aboard. He'd been on that ship before! Like the movie *Avatar*, another version of Adam was already aboard in stasis. Once his consciousness merged with the other version of himself, Adam's mission on Earth was complete.

"When it's my time, once that light shines, I'm gon' fly far away." E.T. had gone home!

I'm still trying to get my head around the intergalactic piece of Adam's story. Adam agreed to come here to gather information as a sacrifice to teach off-planet observers about the human condition. Though it was something he agreed to do; once here, he simply did not fit in. Adam had difficulty living in duality. There was no duality about Adam. What you see is what you get. He needed to get the heck out of here to fulfill his promise to help God and his country.

On January 23, 2011, the night he announced he was going to another realm, Adam was retrieved by the Galactic Federation.

"The Galactic Federation? What is that?" I wondered, typing "Galactic Federation" into Google. *"Holy catfish, Batman! They're like the United Nations!"*

According to Wikipedia, the Galactic Federation is an alliance of extraterrestrial civilizations formed to keep peace within the Milky Way galaxy. According to government officials such as Paul Hellyer, former Canadian minister of national defense; and Haim Eshed, Israel's former head of space security, a "Galactic Federation" not only exists, they rejected Earth's membership. They said we just aren't ready.

"Wake up, people of planet Earth. THE TIME IS NOW. The sand is running out of the hourglass," said Adam, "Time to raise your vibes and suit up."

"What do you mean by suit up?" I asked.

"Time to activate your light body," he said. "When you consciously choose to evolve to a higher state of being, your body holds more light. The more light you hold, the more light you attract. This is not the time to hide your light under a bushel. It's time to suit up and *SHINE! Get your glow on!"*

"If you were picked up by a spacecraft, why didn't they take your body as well?" I asked. "You'd have never known what happened to me," he said. "There would be no book. Believe me, it happens."

"I'm supposed to tell folks that aliens kidnap people?" I asked, ready to argue the point.

"No, you're supposed to tell them I said people are kidnapped by aliens with the government's permission in exchange for technology," said Adam. "Astronauts have seen them. Commercial airline pilots have seen them. The Air Force has seen them. Navy pilots aboard aircraft carriers see more than anyone else. There are UFO bases beneath the ocean floor."

The U.S. Space Force is the sixth independent military branch. Signed into law on December 20, 2019, as part of the 2020 National Defense Authorization Act, the Space Force is tasked with missions and operations *in the rapidly evolving space domain.* Why would the US establish a branch of the military to address something that doesn't exist?

✈ ∴

When Adam was in second grade, his class participated in a book fair. Adam's book, *The Stockton Stormers,* was about an alien

named [1]*Casey who hit a home run out of the universe!*

Score: Love 1
Fear 0

Adam hits a posthumous "home run" out of the universe.

_____

[1] Adam's star is in the constellation Cepheus, the king. King Cepheus = K.C. = Casey.

Chapter 8

Pennies from Heaven

Everything is theoretically impossible
until it is done.
—Robert A. Heinlein

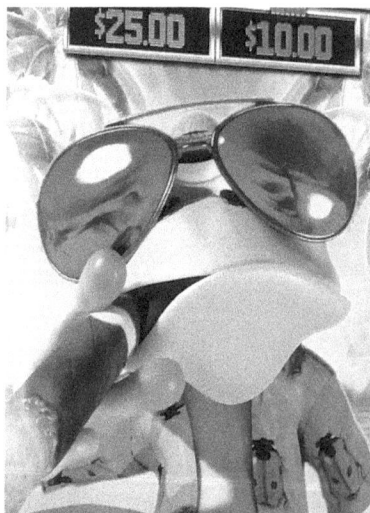

Frog wearing aviator shades
with purple lenses.

Greg and I were married on July 7, 2007 (07/07/07) in Las Vegas. It was the busiest wedding day of the century until August 8, 2008 (08/08/08) came along. In 2018, we went to Jackson Rancheria, a local casino, to celebrate our eleventh anniversary.

I woke up the morning of our anniversary in that half-awake, half-asleep state and asked to connect with Adam. Seconds later, a swirling purple fog appeared in my third eye. The fog settled into the image of a frog wearing aviator sunglasses with purple lenses. I shared the vision with Greg and went back to sleep.

Later that afternoon, while waiting for Greg to make reservations at the seafood buffet, I looked up in jaw-dropping astonishment to see the amphibian from my vision atop a slot machine!

When Greg handed me the buffet tickets, I was so gobsmacked I couldn't speak. The instant I pointed to the frog, the man who'd been playing the slot machine got up and left. I couldn't move. Greg took me by the shoulders and sat me down in his place. Before pulling the handle, I rubbed my palms together the way Adam did when he was manifesting and *cha-ching!* I won $108 in pennies!

11th Anniversary Jackpot.[6]

Remember Christina from the beach in Australia in chapter three, Adam's Ashes? While visiting Sedona, Arizona, she got a tattoo of a horse. She messaged me shortly after. "What's Adam's favorite color?" she asked.

"Black and white and red," I said, "Why do you ask?"

"When I was in Sedona, Adam took me on a wild goose chase. I had no idea what I was looking for until I ended up at a garage sale. Adam pointed to a painting of a zebra. "Look," he said, "it's a striped horse!" Christina bought the painting and shipped it back to Australia.

Christina's mom had difficulty understanding Christina's friendship with Adam. It's not every day your daughter brings home a dead guy. When Christina visited her mom, who lives in the UK, she suggested she read one of my blog posts at www. adamsgift.net. Of all the blog posts she could've read, her mom just happened to read the post about our eleventh-anniversary jackpot. A few weeks later, Mom and Christina traveled to Japan. During their visit, they participated in a trivia game. The question was, "How many stitches on a baseball?"

"A hundred and eight!" shouted Christina's mom.

"How did you know that?" asked Christina.

"Adam told me," she said.

When I wrote the blog post about our eleventh-anniversary jackpot, it felt like I was missing something having to do with the number 108 *when the event that would eventually give it meaning hadn't happened yet!*

When Christina's parents divorced, her mom gave her wedding ring to Christina. Unbeknownst to her mom, Christina lost the ring shortly after receiving it. After their trip to Japan, when Christina's mom visited Christina in Australia, Adam led her mom on a wild goose chase. It ended in a pawn shop in a town she'd never been to before, where she found the wedding ring Christina had lost twenty-plus years earlier!

"If it wasn't the same ring," said Christina, "It was its exact duplicate."

Chapter 9

Duston Saves Grandpa Jim with the Help of Milo and Dr. Oz

> You don't have to be a doctor to help save lives.
> —Dr. Mehmet Oz

Sometimes background noise is just background noise; and sometimes, it's the difference between life and death. One afternoon after work, my thirty-three-year-old nephew, Duston, son of my youngest sister, Rhonda, was sitting at the kitchen table enjoying a heaping bowl of macaroni and cheese. Grandma Joyce and Grandpa Jim were watching Dr. Oz. Today's subject was how to administer CPR.

Grandma Joyce sat with her back to Duston in her carved wooden rocking chair, daily crossword puzzle on her lap. To her right sat Grandpa Jim, less than three feet away from his bride of almost thirty-six years, in his usual spot on the far left side of the well-used maroon leather sofa. Sometimes the details stick in your mind.

Dr. Oz had chosen the perfect guest to demonstrate the potentially lifesaving technique. Milo Ventimiglia plays Jack Pearson, beloved husband and father of three on *This is Us*, one of the most popular shows on TV from 2016 to 2022. Jack's death due to cardiac arrest hit America so hard it likely registered on the Schuman resonance.

Around midnight on a Friday night two weeks before Thanksgiving 2018, Duston woke up to Grandma Joyce's voice. *"Duston! Help! It's Grandpa!"* Duston ran into the bedroom next to his to find Grandpa Jim face down on the carpet where he'd fallen out of bed. Grandpa Jim was a big man. Lucky for him, so was Duston. Rolling Grandpa over, Duston remembered the episode of Dr. Oz.

"Place your hands between the nipples," Oz instructed, "Push down about an inch, and keep it up to the rhythm of "Row, Row, Row Your Boat" until medical help arrives."

Thanks to Duston, Milo, and Dr. Oz, Grandpa Jim made it to the hospital, where he was stabilized. It was touch and go through the weekend, but by Monday, Jim had rallied. Grandpa Jim passed away the following Friday, November 16, 2018, but not before his loved ones could say goodbye.

Greg, Nathan, and I had reservations at an Airbnb in Paso Robles, California, for that weekend. My niece, Donna, was marrying her long-time girlfriend, Monica, in Pismo Beach on Saturday. When I offered to cancel the trip, my mom said, "You should go; we can't make any plans until Monday anyway."

I kept in touch with my mom over the weekend. On Sunday, on the way home, I pulled out my iPhone and told Jim, "It's time you learned how to use the Ghost Radar®. Give me a word to let us know that it's you. "PRINCIPAL," said the Ghost Radar®.

"Wow!" I said, "Great job!" Jim was a retired elementary school principal.

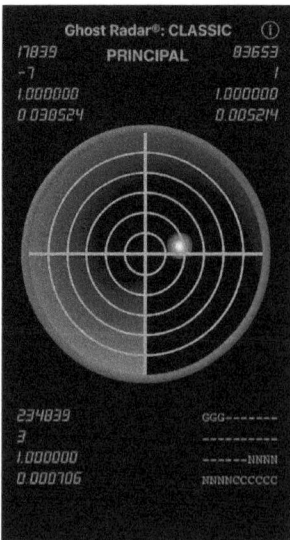

Ghost Radar®, "PRINCIPAL."

"You know how hard it is to convince Mom," I said. "Give us another word and add your initials."

"REPLIED," said the Ghost Radar®, with the letters JJJJJ------------JJJJJ in the lower right-hand corner.

My mom's friend, Linda, also a widow, heard about my Ghost Radar® app. She asked for a demonstration while visiting my mom one day. Jim was born in Oklahoma during the Dust Bowl. As an infant, he lived on grapes. Jim loved nothing better than good conversation and a good meal. He was happiest when he was full as a tick, suffering wonderfully. I asked Jim for a word to identify himself.

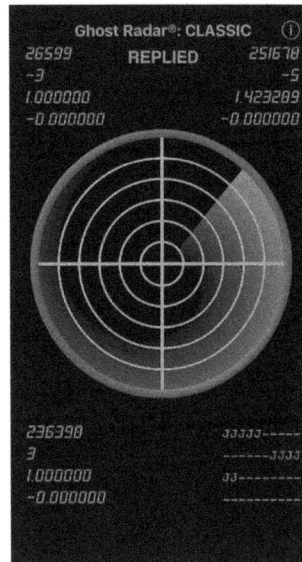

Ghost Radar®, "REPLIED."

"HUNGRY," said the Ghost Radar®.

"No wonder you're hungry," I said, "You haven't eaten since you died." Mom and Jim lived 1.1 miles from Greg and me. I stayed close to my mom between the time Jim died in November 2018, and she died in August 2021. The summer after Jim's death, Greg and I drove up the coast to Oregon for the Fourth of July while my sister, Karen, looked in on Mom. I'd been concerned about the long overdue earthquake in California. Every once in a while, I was reminded of just how overdue it was.

The morning of the Fourth of July, I dreamed about Milo Ventimiglia. We were at an award ceremony for something Milo and I participated in. Whatever it was, it was humanitarian in nature. In the dream, Milo reached into his front pocket and handed me a small box containing a silver turtle on a chain. I knew exactly what the turtle meant at the time. By the time I woke up, I hadn't a clue.

A couple of hours later, at 10:34 a.m., there was an earthquake in the California desert near Ridgecrest, measuring 6.4 on the

Richter scale. When it comes to strength, six tons is twice as heavy as three tons and sixty miles per hour is twice as fast as thirty miles per hour, but a 6.0 earthquake is more than twice the destructive energy of a 3.0 temblor. Imagine the destructive power of a 7.0 earthquake or greater! The state could crack wide open with the number of fault lines in California. Tempted as I am to leave, my loved ones are here, so in California, I remain.

Chapter 10

Daddy Bill

Your pain didn't start with you, but it can end with you.
—Stephanie M. Hutchins, PhD

January 1957

It was a typical Chicago winter, with temperatures ranging from below-freezing to just above freezing. Despite removing her sweater and loosening the collar of her sweat-soaked blouse, nineteen-year-old Joyce was burning up. Three months pregnant, she was still trying to shake off the memory of a dream she had the night before. Heart pounding, there were flashes of strange-looking creatures with a needle. She shivered despite the heat.

Friends from church had come for Sunday Dinner. As Joyce's temperature increased, she started opening windows. First, the kitchen, where the scent of slow-cooked beef wafted skyward through the lace curtains. Dinner was served next to the open dining room window where Fran and Dick Kaufman and their five children sat shivering, still wearing their winter coats.

❄ ☃

I was born in July 1957, in Jeffersonville, Indiana, just across the Ohio River from Kentucky. I would've been born in Chicago, but

my twenty-five-year-old dad, Billy Ray Williams, who managed the employee cafeteria in a shoe factory, had been sent on a short-term assignment to Kentucky. I was six weeks old when we moved back to Chicago, leaving behind the eight-by-thirty-two-foot trailer that served as our home away from home.

Daddy and Mama and Me, Jeffersonville, IN.

My nineteen-year-old mom, Joyce Audrey, was the oldest daughter of a baptize-'em-in-the-river Pentecostal evangelist. The Long Family Gospel Band traveled the south from New Orleans to Georgia and as far north as Chicago. She married my dad at seventeen to spare herself from another road trip.

When handing out cards, they must've been dealing from the bottom of the deck. Billy Ray Williams had a hard life. He was seven when the teacher made him wait out in the hall while the rest of the class celebrated Valentine's Day with cupcakes and candy. All the other little boys and girls wore red, while Billy Ray failed to dress as instructed. He was wearing the same shirt he'd worn the day before. When they were twelve and thirteen, Billy Ray and his younger brother, Bobby Lee, took to running away for the summer

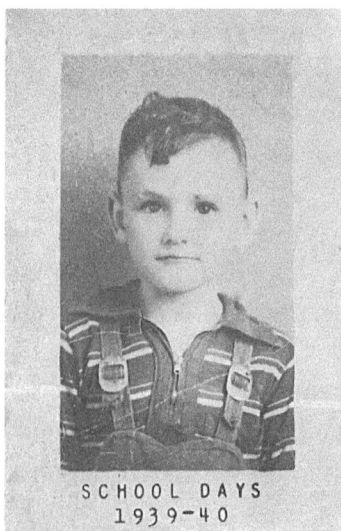

SCHOOL DAYS
1939-40

Billy Ray Williams, age seven.

as soon as school was out. One summer, they made it as far as Texas from their home in Memphis, Tennessee.

Billy Ray was drafted at eighteen and sent back to the front line in Korea.

Billy Ray was sixteen when he lied to an Army recruiter and found himself on the front line in Korea. When a terrified Billy Ray confessed to the lie, he was sent back home. Within days of his eighteenth birthday, Billy Ray was drafted and found himself back on the front line in Korea. This time, he deserted. Billy Ray was sentenced to two years at Leavenworth, Kentucky.

When eighteen-year-old Billy Ray went behind bars, he began a metamorphosis. Twenty-four months later, a confident and charismatic Rev. Billy Ray Williams emerged, newly ordained and filled with the Holy Spirit. Rev. Billy Ray traveled the South preaching the gospel. It was on such a trip that he met evangelist Rev. James I. Long, from Judsonia, Arkansas.

Rev. Long saw opportunity in befriending the handsome young preacher. Fifteen-year-old Joyce would soon be of marrying age. Two years later, when Rev. Long bought a used bloodmobile and prepared to hit the road again, seventeen-year-old Joyce hopped on the back of Billy Ray's motorcycle and headed for Mississippi, where they were married on April 13, 1955.

Like Oscar Diggs, a small-time stage magician and con artist in *The Wizard of Oz*, Billy Ray Williams just wanted *to be somebody*. Sometimes that meant reinventing himself. Lots of times. I have Adam to thank for the ability to forgive my father for my trauma-riddled childhood. Adam helped me, posthumously, to put my dad's life into perspective. I remember the daddy who was my first love. The adoration was mutual.

As soon as I was big enough to hold a telephone, Daddy started calling me from work. He called so often; whenever the phone rang, I'd come running, "Hi, Daddy!"

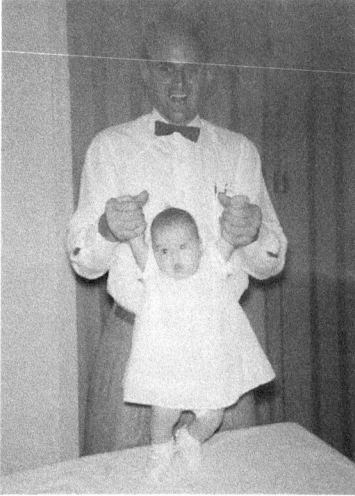

Daddy Bill and me.

My little sisters only remember the man who came home late on school nights, waking us from a sound sleep with his drunken theatrics, ending with our fleeing the scene in our pajamas or Dad's being arrested on the lawn in front of the neighbors.

We moved from Arkansas to Tracy, California, in July 1963, a few days before my sixth birthday. I hadn't been to school a day in my life before entering first grade, but by the end of the school year, I was reading on the fourth-grade level. My mom went to night school to earn her G.E.D. before going to Delta College to earn a degree in business. My dad was a sous chef at the prestigious Tracy Inn.

🥣 👨‍🍳 🍽️

When Karen was born in 1959, we were still living with my dad's parents in Memphis, where we sought shelter after leaving Chicago in the dead of night just ahead of the mob. My dad had been managing a drive-in restaurant in a suburb of Chicago. Once he figured out the carhops were prostitutes working for the chief of police and the mob was laundering money through the restaurant, the fear of returning to Leavenworth began to haunt him.

The chief of police sent a message to Billy Ray, who was becoming more nervous by the day. One Wednesday evening, we came home from church to find every stick of furniture in the house gone besides my crib and the refrigerator. My mom's brand-new wardrobe, the only new clothes she'd ever owned, was also missing. The chief of police's message was clear: *"We know where you live."*

My dad, mom, and I went to stay at her parents' basement apartment in downtown Chicago. When two men in black showed up at the door asking for Billy Ray, he knew they meant business.

"Joyce, grab your purse and the diaper bag and get in the car," he said. "I'm going to the FBI in Memphis."

We moved from Tracy to Stockton, California, in 1965 when a fungus in his thumbnail ended my dad's culinary career. He went to work for a painting contractor in Stockton, where he hung wallpaper and painted houses for a living.

I was fourteen when my parents divorced, and my dad moved to San Francisco. He painted the Golden Gate Bridge twice and several gorgeous old Victorian houses known as Painted Ladies.

My dad would continue to wake me with tearful, drunken phone calls for the rest of his life. I rarely knew where my dad was or whether he was safe. I only knew his deep regret. There was never a time I wasn't in fear, either for my dad or because of him.

Billy Ray Williams was brilliant, talented, and bipolar, a condition he suffered from through no fault of his own. He self-medicated with alcohol and did the best he could to support his family. He had extraordinary ideas worthy of fruition, but he couldn't keep it together long enough to see them through.

Billy Ray moved back to Memphis, where he died of lung cancer at fifty-nine on October 4, 1991. By then, my grandmother Williams had a form of dementia that required twenty-four-hour care. The family thought it was kindest not to tell her.

A few months before he died, I attempted to ask my dad about his final wishes. He was still in denial of his diagnosis and wanted nothing to do with the conversation. I finally got him to bite by saying, "Dad, we're all going to die someday. What would you have done with your remains when the time comes?"

Now that the event was hypothetical, he was willing to entertain the thought.

"I want to be cremated and my ashes spread at my favorite fishing spot," he said, "That way, if I come back as a fish," he joked, "Y'all can visit me."

I made the mistake of repeating that story to my Aunt Beatrice. Horrified, she replied, "It never ceases to amaze me what y'all believe out in California."

Shortly before my dad died, he told his youngest sister, Charlotte, "I know you don't believe I'm going to heaven, but when I get there, I'm going to drop a giant marshmallow on your head."

After Dad died, I asked that his clothes be donated to the Gospel Rescue mission where he volunteered as a cook. Three Sundays later, when Aunt Charlotte returned to church, a bus from the Gospel Rescue mission pulled up outside.

"There was something familiar about those men," she said, "But I couldn't put a finger on it."

When several of them came forward to receive the Holy Ghost, she realized what it was! *Every man on his knees before that preacher was wearing Billy Ray's clothes!*

On the afternoon of my dad's memorial service, I walked into the funeral director's office to ensure Dad's ashes would be ready for pick up at the end of the service. My request was met with an open-mouthed stare. The gentleman stammered in protest that Dad's ashes would, in fact, not be ready until Monday.

With all the assertiveness I could muster, I said, "That won't do. When I selected your funeral home, it was with the understanding that we could release my father's ashes immediately following the service. There are people here who have driven all the way from Alabama to pay their respects, and my sister and I are flying back to California on Monday."

"Let me see what I can do," said the funeral director, who left me standing in his office wondering how in the world I was going to explain this turn of events to my aunts and my grandfather Williams who were already mortified by my dad's decision to be cremated.

A few minutes later, the gentleman returned and said, "You can pick up your father's ashes in my office after the service."

My sister, Rhonda, and I sat beside my mom's youngest sister, Ruth. Rhonda was proud of her newfound sobriety. When she got up to speak, Rhonda's unabashed triumph over alcohol was upstaged by a loud *bang* from somewhere in the building. Startled, I looked at Aunt Ruth. "You know what that sound was," she said. "They just fired up the furnace." It was just like my dad to make one last dramatic entrance before his final curtain call.

When the service ended, I returned to the funeral director's office. As promised, on the corner of his desk sat a box wrapped tightly in white paper with "Billy Ray Williams" across the top, the funeral director nowhere in sight. I cradled my dad's remains against my chest. *The box was searing hot!*

In a panic, I searched for my Aunt Ruth in the lobby. Dad's remains were scorching my bare arms. Transferring the blistering burden to my aunt, I said, "Get this box out of here before one of my dad's sisters touches it. Put it in the van in front of the air conditioner!"

Aunt Ruth, an international fashion model in the '70s, was the image of dignity and grace as she bore my dad's steaming remains out the door in a Dillard's shopping bag.

Thirty-two years later, it occurs to me as I write this, I've finally let the cat out of the bag! *Please, God, don't let one of my dad's relatives read this and suffer a heart attack— death by memoir.*

Following Dad's memorial service, my sister Rhonda and I released Dad's ashes in his brother John's lake. Our sister, Karen, sent a floating wreath we placed in the water with the last of Dad's ashes. As we rowed back to shore, Uncle John looked back over his shoulder and remarked, "Would you look at that? That wreath's acting like it's anchored!" Rhonda and I turned to see Dad's wreath *standing still* despite the current. The water was flowing *around* it.

"That wreath's acting like it's anchored!"
—Uncle John.

The ones to whom his seed gave birth,
Were last to touch him on this earth.
Still warm, our hands held proof. He's gone.
Once Billy Ray, now ash and bone.

Upon the lake, a floating wreath,
Sat anchored while the lake beneath,
Sent gentle waves around the sides.
His favorite place, he now abides.

On my hand a dragonfly,
Dad has come to say goodbye.
As we slowly rowed away,
In my mind, I heard him say,

"Hey girl, everything's copacetic."

Daddy Bill & Mama Joyce–
Mama looks happy.

Shortly before she died, my mom said she'd forgiven my dad for the hardship she endured during their marriage. In hindsight, she saw how hard he struggled to be the man he wanted to be. So softly I could barely hear her; she said, "Your dad had a hard life before I met him. He was always a hard worker and a good provider."

Hurt people, hurt people. Healed people, heal people.

Chapter 11

Mama Joyce

Single moms: You are a doctor, a teacher, a nurse, a maid, a cook, a referee, a heroine, a provider, a defender, a protector, a true superwoman. Wear your cape proudly.
—Mandy Hale

Mama and me on my first birthday.

If we're lucky as children, we live on the precipice of joy and wonder. I lived in such a world. Before moving to California, money was hard to come by, but my sisters and I never went hungry. Until the day of my fourth birthday in July 1961, I felt safe. That was the day my mom and I and my little sisters moved back in with her parents, Grandma and Grandpa Long, so Daddy could take a job as a chef in New Orleans. By then, Mom was five months pregnant with Rhonda.

The job in New Orleans presented the opportunity to save money for a place of our own. My mom, twenty-seven-month-old Karen, and nine-month-old Vicki rode inside the truck with Grandpa. I spent the ninety-eight-mile ride from Memphis,

Tennessee, to Judsonia, Arkansas, in the back of Grandpa's pickup, sandwiched between a box of our belongings and a teenage boy who had no business being left alone with a four-year-old little girl in the back of a pickup.

My dad, who'd always protected me, had just moved seven and a half hours away. Mama was too busy with my little sisters to notice anything unusual. When I hid under the bed that I shared with my mom and sisters, sucking Vicki's bottle, Mama knew what I was doing, but it hadn't occurred to her to wonder why.

Rhonda was born four months later, and we moved back to Memphis in a little house on Edwards Street just down the block from Mom's oldest brother, my Uncle Jimmy. Though we didn't stay in Memphis long, I think it was the longest we'd ever lived anywhere. Before we moved to California, I have more memories of living on Edwards Street than anywhere else. I was the only kid on the block over the age of four who stayed home during the day. All the other kids went to school. You had to pay to go to kindergarten in Memphis in 1962, so I spent most days catching frogs by the creek behind our house.

The summer I turned five, Uncle Jimmy got tuberculosis, and like Grandma Long, he was put in Oakville Sanitorium in Memphis. I'll never forget the day Uncle Jimmy came for a surprise visit and brought me a birthday present. Santa Claus never wrapped our gifts. I think it was the first wrapped present I ever received.

I lifted the little red velvet dress out of the box. It was softer than anything I'd ever felt in my life. Wait a minute—I *had* felt something almost as silky and smooth. Running my hand across the velvet, I said, "Gee, Uncle Jimmy, it's as soft as a frog's belly."

Uncle Jimmy must have gone out back to catch a frog to see for himself. He ran out the back door like his tail was on fire when the police knocked on the front door. They looked in the closets and under the beds and asked my mama a lot of questions about Uncle Jimmy. When I looked up at Mama, the look she gave me nearly turned me to stone. I didn't say a word until the police left.

Oakville Sanitorium is a big building with lots and lots of grass and lots of trees. Lots of trees meant lots of squirrels. You weren't

Oakville Sanitorium,
Memphis, Tennessee.

supposed to shoot and eat them, but that didn't stop Grandpa, even if he was a preacher. There were mouths to feed at home. I don't remember eating squirrel, but chances are I ate it often. I hated seeing the little squirrels get skinned. It upset me so much that my mom threatened her brothers that they better not expose me to any more killing and skinning if they knew what was good for them. Undaunted by her threats, they made me hold the axe when they chopped off the head of a rooster.

While visiting Grandma and Grandpa Long, I'd been inside the house watching my uncles, David and Nathan, through the screen door. They put a big fat rooster in a cardboard box and turned another box upside down on top of it. A half-circle cut out of each box formed a hole the size of the rooster's head. There he stood, as confused as I was, head sticking out of the side of the box.

"What are y'all doing?" I called. That's all the encouragement they needed to invite me to join them. You already know what happened.

"Come on out here," they said, "and we'll show you."

One of them put the axe in my hand; placing both hands over mine, he chopped the rooster's head off. The other removed the top of the box where the headless rooster remained standing. One of the two lifted the

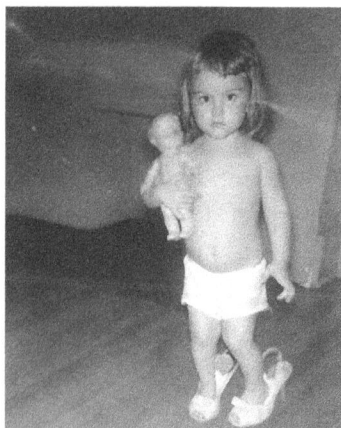

Secondhand Cindy and
One-Eyed Betsy.

78

rooster out of the box and set it down in front of me. As soon as its feet hit the ground, it started running around and around the yard until it finally dropped dead. I ran around and around the yard screaming bloody murder while my uncles roared with laughter.

Soon after I turned five, I was sent to spend a week with my mom's sister, Aunt Lois, in Helena, Arkansas. I didn't think to wonder what was happening at home that my mom didn't want me to witness. You didn't do or say anything around little Cindy that you didn't want reported or repeated. I'd never slept away from home without my dad or mom. I was so homesick; I didn't know what to do. Aunt Lois attempted to fill the giant hole that began growing inside me the instant the front door closed and my daddy went home without me.

"What can I get for you, Miss Cindy?" asked Aunt Lois with genuine concern. She was in the kitchen with cookies and ice cream at her disposal. No matter what I asked for, no sooner did she deliver it than I'd burst into tears again.

"I want orange juice!" I cried. Preparing the orange juice, I overheard Aunt Lois, who was pretty frustrated by then, say under her breath, "I'd like to put some A-R-C-E-N-I-C in it."

I watched her like a hawk. The instant she set the glass on the table, I burst into tears. "You didn't put any A-R-C in it!" I cried.

"What's the matter with you?" she asked.

"I miss my father-in-law!" I bawled.

"You don't have a father-in-law," she said, bemused.

My grandfather, Rev. James I. Long, who still lived in Judsonia, was dispatched to retrieve me and take me home to Memphis. Grandpa spent the entire trip from Helena to Memphis indoctrinating me into his religion. I repeated Grandpa's sermon to my sisters the next morning at breakfast. Three-year-old Karen was all ears. "Grandpa said If you do anything bad," I warned, "the devil will put you in his fire."

"I know why the devil's so mean," Karen offered. "He misses

his mommy." Mama had taken a job on the graveyard shift at a factory while I was in Helena.

Daddy was still working in New Orleans. We had a babysitter during the day and had to be quiet while Mama slept. Mama seemed sad all the time. The only thing that made her happy was the mail. The rent check hadn't arrived from New Orleans for several months. We were going to have to move back to Judsonia.

One day while she was sleeping, I collected all the mail on the block and brought it home to Mama. I was confused when I didn't get the reaction I expected. "Why, Cindy," she cried. "Where did you get all this mail?" My poor mom had to redeliver the mail with me and all three little sisters in tow, in addition to her job on the graveyard shift.

For the most part, my mom raised us by herself. My dad did the best he could. He could always find a job but couldn't always keep it. The alcohol he used to self-medicate turned him into somebody else. By the time we were teenagers, Dad was totally out of the picture. Any money he sent was given to us girls. Mom had supported us on her own, selling real estate since I was about eleven. She'd never counted on or received any income from my dad or anyone else that she didn't earn.

When my mom married at seventeen, she hadn't graduated from high school yet or gotten her driver's license. The oldest of seven children, from the age of seven, her primary responsibility had been taking care of her younger brothers and sisters while her mother nursed the baby, whichever one it was until it got bigger and became my mom's responsibility. Between babies, according to my mom, her mama went to church with her daddy to keep an eye on the ladies who were keeping an eye on Grandpa.

By the age of twenty-three, my mom had given birth to four girls within four years and four months. I can't even imagine how it must have felt every time she landed right back on her parents' front porch with another baby. My dad tried to be a good husband

and father. How tempting it must have been for the charismatic young sous chef.

Like a moth to a flame, waitresses had been attracted to Billy Ray since we lived in Chicago. They were no less ardent in New Orleans. Once Daddy forgot to remove the evidence from the floorboard of the car. *"If only he'd used protection when he came home,"* thought my mom, who by then had too many of Billy Ray's kids to wish him harm.

Once we moved to Tracy, California, and Daddy's drinking and carousing continued, Mom began to plan her escape. She got her driver's license, earned her high school diploma at night school, and began driving the short distance to Stockton a couple of nights a week to attend Delta College. She earned a degree in business and got her real estate license within five years of arriving in California. She got her broker's license and opened her own office with a partner shortly thereafter. By then, we had moved to Stockton.

Joyce Audrey Williams

When the four of us girls were teenagers, Mom made sure we were well acquainted with Planned Parenthood. She wanted none of her daughters to follow in her footsteps. Vicki ultimately had eight children, two sons, and six daughters. Only the first one was a surprise, as firstborns often are. I had two sons, Karen had a son and a daughter, and Rhonda had one son. Mom loved every one of her daughters and every one of her grandchildren and great-grandchildren. She never stopped supporting Planned Parenthood.

Mom not only donated money every month, she devoted hundreds of hours shielding frightened clients of Planned Parenthood with an umbrella as they made their way into the clinic, often with a crowd of Christians holding signs, shouting threats, and quoting Bible verses. Mom could match the Bible thumpers quote for quote. In fact, she enjoyed it. All those years of arguing scripture with Grandpa over the kitchen table finally paid off.

My mom was the original Wonder Woman. She was emailing jokes to friends and family the afternoon of her second mastectomy, five years after the first one. Mom's philosophy was, "Shit happens. Deal with it." *That was her life.* Shit happened, and she dealt with it. Mom's health began to decline shortly after Jim died in November 2018. Fortunately for Greg and me, she only lived a mile away.

When we started bringing dinner to Mom's house in the evenings instead of eating at home, the first thing we did was set a place for Jim at the head of the table. In Jim's chair sat a life-sized teddy bear. Mom enjoyed reminiscing after dinner. Once I realized she was on a roll, I'd hit the "record" button on my cell phone.

Mom and Jim's birthdays were two years and two days apart. When she was sixteen, Mom and her cousin, Helen, enjoyed walking around downtown Memphis on the weekends. One Saturday, Mom giggled as they walked past the Ellis Auditorium at the corner of Poplar and Front Street. "Look at that," she said, pointing to the marquee. "Somebody named *Ellis* is fighting at the *Ellis* Auditorium."

My future stepdad, eighteen-year-old Jim Ellis, a golden gloves boxer, won that match at the Ellis Auditorium in Memphis while attending Harding University in Searcy, Arkansas, two hours west of Memphis.

Mom and Jim met at a dance class at Delta College in Stockton on a Saturday morning in 1981. Jim was talked into taking the class by a friend who convinced the newly divorced school principal that it was time he learned to dance. Mom just wanted to dance. When she was in her forties, Mom, my sisters, and I could light it up. Our favorite song was "We Are Family" by

Sister Sledge. Too bad they didn't have cell phones back then, or I could share a video of the best-looking butts in the house doing the bump. Folks often thought Mom was our sister. If one of us so much as opened our mouths to correct them, we'd get kneed in our fine-looking ass.

Mom and Jim were married on Christmas Eve 1982 before the fireplace in the home they shared. Mom's friend, Judge Sandra Smith, officiated. Jim's best man was Todd Anton, the superintendent of the school district where Jim was a school principal. Mom's maid of honor was her best friend, Linda Bacani, a surgical nurse. Six months pregnant with Adam, I wore a dark green corduroy jumper. String some lights around me, and I could have been mistaken for the Christmas tree. Mom and Jim were happily married a month short of thirty-six years.

Joyce Audrey was a beautiful, brown-eyed brunette with a mischievous smile, a heart of gold, a great sense of humor, and a potty mouth when the appropriate lexicon failed to suit her requirements. A prolific letter writer, Mom authored a plethora of letters to the editor of the *Stockton Record* over the years. She was an avid reader, a Toastmaster, a champion of women and children, a volunteer for her political party, a devoted wife, sister, friend, mother of four, grandmother of thirteen, and as of July 2023, great-grandmother of eleven. Her humble beginnings never forgotten; mom never turned away a soul in need. She was truly one of a kind.

The Long children: Ruth, Jimmy, Joyce holding Nathan, Lois, and David.

From my mom's journal on February 1, 2007:

> Aunt Bessie was buried last Thursday on a bright sunny winter day. It was fitting that it was winter. Her life had run a full course of ninety-five years. She wanted to go and was eager for the exit. The sun could only have shown that day to bless her rest because she brought lightness and gladness to so many hearts.
>
> I looked at her lying there, always slender, now thin, looking so like her mother, except for that jutting chin denoting a stubborn streak. Her thin, small hands, work-worn, never pretty, had the Tapley shape which had raised four children, Catherine, Patsy, Gerald Don, and last Lowell. She raised four grandchildren, Larry, Dennis, Michael,

and Donna Williams, and nurtured countless other grandchildren, great-grandchildren, great-great-grandchildren, nieces, nephews, and their friends and their children.

I never heard her complain about her lot, although she lived her whole married life in a shack on a hill in North Central Arkansas. She always said she had the best view around and a wonderful natural spring for water. I don't think she had an inside toilet until her kids moved an old mobile home onto the property after Uncle Oscar died twenty-nine years ago. She never made us kids wait until the adults ate, as was the custom then when the table was too small to seat everyone. She made us a place or let us eat first, knowing kids have too much to do to linger at the table.

Joyce and Lois Long at eight and six years old, best friends to the end.

We loved to go up there in the summer. She would give all of us kids, usually six, seven, or more, three-pound lard buckets and tell us to go pick her some berries, and she would make us a pie. We would be gone till noon, playing, climbing trees, wading in the stream that flowed down from the spring, and, yes, picking several buckets of blackberries.

Meanwhile, she had gotten her work done and made lunch. We called it dinner. Another carefree afternoon wandering her farm or playing games, and back for supper at which time we would have blackberry pie or cobbler, and she would have canned several jars of the excess berries.

We didn't realize we were working. Then evenings outside, chasing fireflies and telling ghost stories. So different from our city lives where we couldn't leave the yard, couldn't have friends over, and an endless responsibility for the younger children and the babies.

Aunt Bessie was always cheerful and smiling. Although her life was hard, I never heard her say a harsh word about her husband. Her mother and sisters called him a lazy ne'er-do-well and prefixed almost every reference to her as "Poor Bessie." They both seemed content on their hill, while all her sisters' favorite pastime seemed to be heaping calumny on their husbands and brothers-in-law. Their righteousness was demonstrated by pointing out the faults of others. Hers was lived in the service of others.

The last time I visited Aunt Bessie, she had dozens of family pictures on her walls of children, grandchildren, and great-grandchildren, and she bragged on them all. She reminisced about her marriage to Uncle Oscar when they went looking for a justice of the peace in the middle of the night. Their car had gotten stuck, and being out overnight and unmarried would have set tongues a-wagging. They were married in the glow of the headlights.

I was only mad at Aunt Bessie once when I was four, and I had picked five pounds of cotton in a tow-sack she strapped over my shoulder. I kept reminding her they owed me five cents, a penny a pound. The anger was generated when

I overheard Aunt Bessie whisper to Uncle Oscar behind her hand, "Give her five pennies instead of a nickel so she'll think she has a lot of money." Oh, the humiliation that she would think I was ignorant enough to believe five pennies was greater than a nickel! Did she think I was as ignorant as the rest of those snot-nosed kids? Please!

Oh, well, you can't stay mad at someone whose hot biscuits are legendary, and no one could quite duplicate, and every humble bite you ate at her table surpassed the efforts of great chefs because it was served with a generous spirit and a glad heart.

Hers was the only eulogy I ever heard where the minister seemed to share the loss of the family. He'd officiated at the funerals of her husband and daughter and grandson and seemed to know and love her personally. So different from some who obviously never met the deceased. She is buried near her husband, son, and daughter. May she rest in peace.

Mama and me at my wedding in 1981, Sunnyvale, California.

For most of my life, I considered my mother my best friend. There was nothing I couldn't tell her. Things changed after Adam died, and our belief systems began to clash. Mom was delightful company when she wasn't overwhelmed by other people's problems. She thinks setting boundaries is selfish. We only lived a mile apart. I think setting boundaries is mandatory.

A few years before she died, Mom was out for a walk and dropped by unexpectedly. I offered her coffee and sat back down where I'd been working on *Adam's Gift*. "Are you still working on that book?" she asked. "Yes," I said, "and I have a blog."

"I understand it's cathartic," she remarked, "but don't you think your time would be better spent serving children?"

"Let me see if I've got this right," I said. "You see no value in my writing other than catharsis, and you think I should do for free what I was paid very well to do before retiring?"

Adam's Gift: The Blog

Adam's Gift–The Blog.

Mom and I both suffered the misfortune of having to wear glasses with Coke bottle bottom lenses. Mom's huge brown eyes grew even larger when they met mine. Stormy with chances of thunder. That was the one and only time I ever invited my mom to leave. I was afraid of saying something I'd regret.

October 2020

Greg and I were at my mom's house enjoying a glass of wine after dinner when Jim's sister, Jean, who typically moves at a snail's pace, flew through the front door.

"You guys! Get out here! You have to see this!" Jean had been standing out front smoking a cigarette when two orange orbs appeared out of nowhere. Greg grabbed his iPhone, and we joined her.

Easily visible against the clear night sky, the bright orange orbs grew bigger, then smaller. One sped up. The other slowed down.

When one shot up and out of eyesight, another appeared from the side. We watched until the last of the orbs disappeared over the western horizon.

As we sat at the kitchen table watching the video, Mom, who'd been sitting with her back to us in her rocking chair a few feet away, said, "Aliens are real. They kidnap you, and they take you on their ships, and they do things to you."

Greg, Jean, and I sat in stunned silence.

Orange orbs over I-5 freeway, Stockton, CA, October 1, 2020, 8:26 pm

Did she just say what we think she said?

I thought of the dream Mom had when she was three months pregnant with me, of freezing Fran and Dick Kaufman and their five kids in her dining room in January 1957 when she opened all the windows during a nuclear hot flash. The night before, she had dreamed about strange creatures doing something to her with a needle.

I waited a few days for a private moment to ask Mom about the remark. She looked at me like I had two heads and said, "I never said any such thing."

When we moved to California, the number of my tribe dropped down to six. I missed the rest of my family terribly. My dad's oldest sister, Aunt Dolores, lived with Uncle Wally and their five kids in Mississippi. We went to see them the summer I turned seven. The day we arrived; Aunt Dolores was making corn on the cob. I had a loose tooth I was determined to pull before dinner.

"I'll take care of it," offered Uncle Wally, who tied one end of a string to my tooth and the other to the doorknob and slammed the door. My only concern was whether the Tooth Fairy knew Uncle Wally's address. I returned to school that fall wearing some of the cutest outfits I'd ever owned, thanks to my cousins Carrie and Sherry's hand-me-downs.

Cindy Williams, fourth grade, Pulliam Elementary School.

I don't remember when it started, but I began having a recurring dream about visiting Aunt Dolores and Uncle Wally and my cousins Diana, Donald, Carrie, Sherry, and Gary. In the dream, they lived in a different house. This one was across from a lake with a front porch half the length of the house.

I went back to Arkansas in September 2021, a month after my mom died, for a family reunion on my dad's side at the home of my cousin Gary and his wife, Elisa. It was wonderful seeing my cousins again. My cousin Donald looks just like my daddy, his Uncle Billy. Uncle Wally was the picture of health at ninety, still rosy-cheeked and standing tall and as much a character as he ever was.

My cousins and I made plans to get together for dinner at Carrie's house the night before I left for California. We were eating dinner at a table half the length of Carrie's front porch when I suddenly realized where I was. There was the lake across the street!

It was the house in my dream!

In Carrie's laundry room is the cutest piece of art. It's nothing but a window frame, but I found it charming. "Uncle Billy gave that to Mama," she said, "when he painted the University of Central Arkansas in Conway. They replaced some of the windows in McAlister Hall."

When I took photos of the house in my dream, the light play was incredible, with rays shooting down from the heavens.

"Hi Daddy! Hi Mama! Hi Aunt Dolores!"

Chapter 12

Cindyana Jones and the Ain't-No-Hand-Me-Down-Adam Skull

> Cindy, you and your family have made my hair stand
> on end more than anything in the known Universe.
> —Carolyn Ford, guardian of Einstein, the
> Ancient Crystal Skull of Consciousness

The Adam Skull and Einstein, the Ancient Crystal Skull of Consciousness.

It began with a Skype session with my intuitive friend Kerry Kennedy in the spring of 2016. Kerry had just finished her shift as a barista in Scotland. It was around seven in the evening there and eleven in the morning in California, where I sat with my laptop, enjoying our visit. "One of your relatives is here," she offered.

Kerry is magical. *I've seen orbs stream out of her throat on video.*

"His name starts with a J. He's singing to you."

"What's he saying?" I asked.

"He's singing, 'Now that your rose is in bloom, you'll shine a light on the gray.'" "It could be my Uncle Jimmy," I guessed.

"He's calling you Nancy Drew," said Kerry. "Who's Nancy Drew?" Thirty-two-year-old Kerry had never heard of the teenage detective. I didn't know what to make of either the song or the comparison to Nancy Drew, so I did what I'd been doing since Adam's transition and filed it away in the back of my mind with a lot of other strange phenomena that didn't make sense.

What do Harrison Ford, David Blaine, and I have in common? Don't know? Neither did I, and it about drove me *batshit*. Six months after my visit with Kerry, in September 2016, I dreamed I was at Harrison Ford's house. It felt like a holiday.

Harrison and I were seated across from each other on light-colored sofas arranged in an L-shape. There was a cube-shaped object in my hands with wires sticking out of one end. When Harrison leaned forward to reach for the cube, his hand touched one of the wires, completing the circuit, and *Zap! That thing shocked the crap out of both of us!*

It was so totally unexpected. He found the look on my face as funny as I found the look on his, and we couldn't stop laughing. We were rolling side to side against the back of our respective sofas, tears of laughter rolling down our cheeks. Once I collected myself, I picked up an empty hors d'oeuvres plate from the chunky wooden coffee table before me and headed for the kitchen.

When I entered the kitchen, there were three women standing across the room between the oven and an island in the center of the room, blocking the exit. On the island were two bowls of fruit and a rack of pots and pans hanging from the ceiling. The kitchen was white, and the sink was in the far corner of the room beneath a window near where the women stood talking. The women were still deep in conversation when the plate was dry, so I went out the same way I came in. Besides there being a spiral staircase just outside the kitchen, that's the last I remember of the dream.

That covers Harrison and me, but where does David Blaine fit in? *Glad you asked.* David Blaine is an illusionist who's done several TV specials. *Beyond Magic* aired in 2016. Among other celebrities, it features Katie Perry, Aaron Paul, Bryan Cranston, Will and Jada Pinckett Smith's family and Harrison Ford. When Harrison Ford picked a card, committed it to memory, and put it back, Blaine told him his card had left the deck.

After Harrison searched the deck to no avail, Blaine advised him to grab a piece of fruit they could open. Harrison handed him an orange.

Blaine asked him to reveal the card he'd drawn.

"The nine of hearts," says Harrison, watching Blaine cut open the orange to reveal the nine of hearts. Once Harrison caught his breath, he said, *"Get the fuck outta my house. OK?"*

It was New Year's Eve 2016, and I wanted something especially fun to watch, so I chose the David Blaine special. Imagine my surprise when during the scene with Harrison Ford, *the very kitchen I'd washed my plate in three months ago appeared on my eighty-five-inch big screen!*

On the morning of my mom's seventy-ninth birthday, January 28, 2017, I awoke with my elusive great-great-grandfather Jones on my mind. Had my maternal great-grandfather taken the name of his father instead of his mother, my mother's maiden name would've been Jones. Why was I thinking of him? Then it occurred to me that he might be the relative whose name starts with a J who popped in during my visit with Kerry Kennedy last spring. I thought of the

David Blaine, Real or Magic?

David Blaine special
Real or Magic.[8]

dream again. I asked myself, "What do I think of when I think of Harrison Ford?" *Indiana Jones!*

I was born in Indiana. By rights, I'm a Jones. *Cindyana Jones!* I tried it aloud, "Cindyana Jones." *That's me! I'm Cindyana Jones!* I recognized my essence in the sound of the name. *The dream is about finding my archetype!* When Cindyana Jones goes into the cave, *she doesn't come out without the crystal skull.* That explains why it feels like I'm being sent on one spiritual wild-goose chase after the other!

That still leaves the mystery of the identity of my great-great-grandfather Jones. The Harrison Ford dream compelled me to send a DNA sample to ancestry.com. No one in the family knew Jones's first name. Somebody knew he was in town on business.

When Jones met my great-great-grandmother, Jane DeLong, it was love at first sight. Jones, who was from Texas, promised to return and marry Jane. Neither had any idea Jane was pregnant. By the time Jones returned, Jane had already had the baby, given up on his ever coming back, and married someone else. When the baby was born, Jane DeLong removed the "De" from her last name and gave it to the baby, christening him, "Willie Dee Long."

The family of Willie Dee and Lillie Lee Long.

Shortly after his eighteenth birthday, Willie Dee was walking down the street when a shiny black car rolled up beside him. Its Texas oil-rich occupant invited Willie to go for a ride. Jones introduced himself and offered to leave Willie his fortune if Willie would take his name. It was a "Luke, I am your father" moment. Having grown up a bastard in the late 1800s, a furious Willie Dee told Jones to keep his money, a decision he grew to regret.

Willie Dee Long fathered ten children in the early 1900s. All ten of Willie Dee's children grew up and had children of their own. Those children had children who had children who had children. That's a lot of Longs who should be Joneses.

By then, I'd discovered, via the DNA test, that my fifth great-grandfather on the Williams side's name was Geoffrey Jones. *I'm a Jones on both my mother's and father's sides.*

A hint provided by ancestry.com's algorithm led me to a social security record entitling Wille Dee's mother, Jane Long, to the social security pension of "Dave Jones." During our visit with David Bowie on our YouTube channel, *Chillin' with Adam,* Bowie said he had a surprise for me. When I said I couldn't wait to find out what it was, there was an EVP at 31:33. You can hear Bowie say, "Ask me."

What was Bowie's surprise? He said his real name isn't Bowie. "I made that up. My real name is David Jones." Bowie hadn't explicitly stated that he and my great-great-grandfather had the same first and last name, so until I found the social security record with the name Dave Jones, I thought they shared just the same last name. With that, the case of *Cindyana Jones and the Missing Great-Great Grandfather* was solved. Case closed.

David Bowie: "Ask me."

Chillin' with Adam: EVP with David Bowie.[9]

Former Navy Communications Officer Ron Lederer is an expert in deciphering EVPs. Once Ron learned about Adam, he invited him to speak up. "Give me a code word or any word to show that you can communicate. Any word," said Ron.

"Superstud," said Adam. EVPs are usually distorted, but anyone who's ever heard Adam's voice can attest *that EVP sounds just like Adam!"*

Blog: Elvis: Adam EVP "Super Stud"

Blog post with Adam's EVP, "Superstud."[10]

In January 2019, I was at my mom's house working on the memorial handout for Jim's celebration of life. Around four o'clock, I received a message from Carolyn Ford, guardian of Einstein, the Ancient Crystal Skull of Consciousness. As mentioned earlier in the book, Greg and I met Carolyn at the Wesak festival in Mt. Shasta, California, in May 2011, four months after Adam's transition.

Several months later, Carolyn and her partner, Ron, let us know they would be coming to the Center for Sacred Studies in Guerneville, California, in September and would like to get together if we were interested. We met Carolyn and Ron in Guerneville where we acquired the first of our family of crystal skulls, Adam and Eve, a three-pound golden citrine and a four-pound amethyst we'd admired in Mt. Shasta in May.

The capsulized version of the message from Carolyn was that she was showing a client some crystal skulls when the client asked Carolyn to tell her about the twenty-three-pound smoky quartz crystal skull sitting before her. Carolyn said he was new, having just arrived in a barrel with some other skulls. "What's his name?" asked the customer.

Carolyn meditates with each skull to learn their names and familiarize herself with their properties. "Let me ask him," she replied. "What's your name?" asked Carolyn, posing the question directly to the crystal skull.

"I am Adam," said the skull, and just like that, she sensed Adam's energy. It was as though he were standing right before her, arms folded across his chest like a genie. That's exactly how Adam is standing in the last photo taken of him on New Year's Eve 2010.

Carolyn added, "I just had to contact you. I can feel him all around me. *Yikes!* Call me if you're around," and left her phone number.

When I called Carolyn, she said the Adam Skull arrived in a barrel with some other skulls. She had just enough time to unpack them when her client inquired about the twenty-three-pound smoky quartz claiming to be my son. I already had a golden citrine Adam skull, and crystal is expensive.

I asked Carolyn what the skull meant by, "I am Adam." How can that skull *be* my son?

"The skull *isn't* your son," explained Carolyn, *"Your son has embodied the skull with his consciousness."*

"Why didn't he embody his consciousness into the three-pound Adam skull I already have?" I reasoned.

"Ain't no hand-me-down-Adam," interjected Adam.

Whether or not I understood the *"how"* behind Carolyn's story, I recognized Adam's vernacular.

"Ain't no hand-me-down Adam." Only Adam would come up with an answer like that.

Adam had always been a divergent thinker. One day in kindergarten, all the kids in the morning and afternoon classes made snowmen. When I walked in to talk with Mrs. Malde, Adam's kindergarten teacher, all the little clay snowmen were lined up on the back counter. "Can you tell which one is Adam's?" asked Mrs. Malde.

They were all the way across the room. I squinted, then laughed out loud. There were over sixty snowmen on that counter, but only one was wearing a ten-gallon cowboy hat. The next time they played with Play-Doh, Adam came home and announced, "We played with Play-Doh again today." When I asked what he made, he offered, "It was pink. I made a penis."

When I went to the school to apologize to Mrs. Malde, Adam was sitting on a bench blowing up a balloon. "Oh, please!" said Mrs. Malde, "Do you know how many Play-Doh penises I've seen in my life?" Once again, I was secure in Mrs. Malde's good graces when I turned around to see Adam put the balloon on the bench and sit on it. "Plthffffffttt!"

Fart Spelling Bee

"Fart Spelling Bee."[11]

"He's a genius!" cried Mrs. Malde, throwing her arms up in celebration of Adam's creativity. "I want to show you something,"

Adam and Mrs. Malde

she said. She went into the classroom and returned with a piece of paper. Adam's name was at the top. "This is Adam's work," she said, holding up a math sheet with ten addition problems at the top and ten subtraction problems at the bottom. "Adam was the first to finish, but he added all twenty problems. I pointed to the subtraction problems at the bottom and told him to correct them. He returned thirty seconds later. As you can see," she said, pointing to the subtraction problems, "He crossed all the minus signs."

When the Adam Skull said he wasn't "no hand-me-down," I knew it was Adam. I didn't know *how* it was Adam, but I knew it *was* Adam. Using the Ghost Radar® app, I asked Adam to give me one word describing his relationship to the Adam Skull and to put his initials on it. The word he gave me was, "UNION," followed by six capital As. Union is the act of uniting two or more things.

I was despondent when Carolyn told me the price of the Adam Skull. The thought of someone else with the skull my son's consciousness embodied was unthinkable, but I couldn't afford a twenty-three-pound crystal skull. Just as Einstein was meant to be with Carolyn, she knew the Adam Skull was meant to be with me.

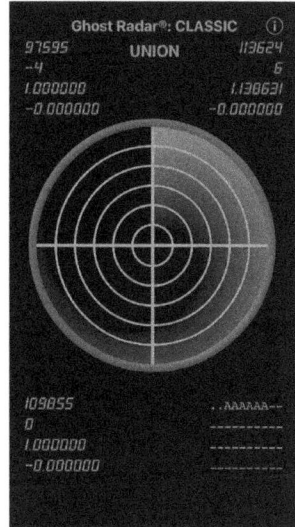

Ghost Radar®, "UNION," with six capital As.

"You're a unique and rare family," said Carolyn, "Einstein said we are in service to your higher expression. We'll make it work."

Adam with his last Christmas gift to me, *"Tear that motherfucker open and read it!"*

Adam's last gift to me was laser stars that turn my bedroom ceiling into a cerulean sea of night sky. I'd never seen Adam so excited about a gift. For the first time, all our kids were together for Christmas. My younger son, Nathan, had just returned from North Carolina, where he spent six months getting clean and sober.

Greg's daughter, Ashley, and his son, Stephen, were there. Adam's gifts were exquisitely wrapped in shiny white paper embossed with black velvet. The black and white bows on top were handmade.

"You'll never guess what it is," Adam teased, rubbing his palms together in anticipation.

"Why can't I guess it?" I asked.

"Because it's something you just can't *give* somebody," he reasoned.

"What did you get me, Adam?" I asked. *"The universe?"*

Adam and I had been sitting side-by-side on the floor. He shot up like a jack-in-the-box, grabbed the gift, and said, *"Tear that motherfucker open and read it!"*

Inside the box was a laser star projector. Outside the box were the words, *THE UNIVERSE IN A BOX.*

That was the Saturday before Adam's last Christmas. The Sunday before Christmas was the day Adam and I went to church together. As I mentioned in the introduction, going to church wasn't a regular event in our family, so when Adam suggested it, I asked why he wanted to go. "To get some comfort," he replied. Adam kept an hourglass in the center of a large round coffee table in his apartment. I had no way of knowing the sand was running out.

I suggested we go to Unity, where Adam had promised to help God and his country. On the Sunday before Adam's last Christmas, an angel appeared with its wings over Adam and me while the congregation's heads were bowed in prayer. Antoinette Celle, the woman sitting directly behind us, could hardly believe her eyes.

The angel's appearance at church that day was intended to provide comfort once Adam transitioned, but I didn't learn of the angel's visitation until after Adam's memorial service in February. Antoinette was concerned that I might think she was crazy. However long it took her to deliver the message, I'll be forever grateful to Antoinette for sharing.

Crystal serves as an amplifier. Simply being in the presence of the Adam Skull increases your frequency. Made of smoky quartz, the Adam Skull also provides protection, disperses fear, lifts depression, relieves stress and anxiety, promotes positive thinking, and enhances spiritual growth.

The Adam Skull wearing a red Angels ball cap.

How Adam managed to program the twenty-three-pound crystal skull would remain a mystery until three years later, when the explanation would come from a most unlikely source.

In January 2022, I became a QHHT® practitioner. The Quantum Healing Hypnosis Technique developed by Dolores Cannon is a healing method that employs the use of past-life regression to inform present life issues. One of my first QHHT® clients, whom I'll call Dion, was a handsome young black man in his late twenties. I met Dion through my longtime hair stylist, Selinda. She'd been telling each of us about the other for months. She was certain we shared common interests. She was right! Before Dion's QHHT® session, we were chatting with my husband, Greg, when Dion remarked that the two of us felt so familiar. He pointed to a photo of Adam.

"Who's that?" he asked.

"That's my son, Adam, who transitioned," I said.

"He looks familiar too!" said Dion.

When I suggested we ask his subconscious if we'd known each other in a past life, he agreed. Under hypnosis, Dion confirmed, "The four of us were siblings in Atlantis."

"What do you do in Atlantis?" I asked.

"I'm a scientist," he said.

"What do I do?" I asked,

"You're a cellular biologist," he answered.

"What about Greg?" I asked.

"He's an educator."

He added, "For Adam, I'm getting *beloved brother.* Adam and I were especially close."

"What did Adam do during that lifetime?" I queried.

"Adam was a keeper of knowledge," said Dion.

Before the destruction of Atlantis, knowledge was programmed into crystals and hidden in Egypt and Arkansas.

"Cindyana Jones & The Adam Skull[11]."

Once in possession of the Adam Skull, I considered what to call it. I like the Ain't-No-Hand-Me-Down-Adam Skull. It showcases Adam's sense of humor.

"Rearrange the letters," said Adam.

Grabbing a piece of paper, in all caps, I wrote, AIN'T NO HAND ME DOWN ADAM. Rearranging the letters, I came up with, ADAM IN THE NOW AND DNA.

The only two letters remaining form the primordial sound that created the Universe, *"OM!"*

"Hey, Mom," said Adam, "What's another word for gift?"

That's easy, I thought. "Present?"

"What's another word for present?" he queried.

"Here," I said, thinking of roll call in elementary school.

"That's right," he said, *"Adam's here!"*

Rainbow-shaped "third eye" projecting from the Adam Skull.

Chapter 13

David Duchovny, Why Don'tcha Love Me?

There are no limitations unless you create
them yourselves. Anything is possible.
You are only limited by your own imagination.
—Dolores Cannon

In February 2022, I was doing my QHHT® (Quantum Healing Hypnosis Technique) internship when I had a dream about David Duchovny. Not *that* kind of dream. The house was dark, but for the light coming from my laptop. *There was someone sitting in my chair.* It took a minute, but I recognized David Duchovny from *The X-Files. What is he doing on my laptop?* His attention glued to the screen; my presence went unnoticed. Leaning forward, eyes scanning back and forth, whatever Duchovny was reading had his full attention. In a flash of intuition, I realized he was reading my QHHT® session notes!

"*He's trying to steal my X-files!*"

"I don't have any "X" files," I mused. When I use the term "X" file, "X" is for something highly unusual that would be of interest to others. The QHHT® sessions I'd done so far were compelling but nothing I'd consider remarkable. The very next morning, I got my first "X" file. I love the synchronicity! The David Duchovny dream served as a harbinger of more "X" files to come.

During a QHHT® session, when a client experiences a past life, I ask them to describe their feet. Skin color, gender, the size of the foot, shoes, or no shoes; you can learn a lot from a pair of feet. When I asked a client I'll call Cynthia to look at her feet, she was very sure of herself.

"I'm wearing black shoes. I am Helena. I know who I am."

Helena Blavatsky was a Russian mystic who held séances in her home. She gained an international following when she co-founded the Theosophical Society in 1875. It's my understanding that when Greg and I were married in a past life, we attended one of Helena Blavatsky's séances.

Helena's biographer, Peter Washington, described her as noisy, humorous, and witty, unpretentious, and sometimes crude, scandalous, impulsive, and capricious. Though warmhearted and welcoming, Helena was fonder of animals than people.

Considered an eccentric who abided by no rules except her own, Helena couldn't be more different than Cynthia. Though Cynthia is very interested in spirituality, she is neither loud nor unconcerned about rules or societal norms. She's married with children and leading a relatively normal life this time around.

I regressed Cynthia to the day of the séance held in Helena's home.

"You are here," said Helena, referring to Greg and me in the past life we shared with Helena.

"I am," I confirmed.

Referring to the past life husband who accompanied me to the seance —it was actually *his* idea; I went reluctantly, I said, "Did you meet my husband?"

As Cynthia arrived for her session, Greg was leaving, and I introduced them. "I met him this morning," said Helena, "as he was walking out the door."

During a QHHT® session in Jacksonville, Arkansas, in the summer of 2022, with a client I'll call Rosie, we met Aimee Crocker, daughter of Edwin Bryant Crocker, a California Supreme Court justice and founder of the Crocker Art Museum in Sacramento.

Aimee is fondly remembered as a bohemian, a mystic, an American princess, and author with a delightful sense of humor and a tattoo or two most folks weren't aware of. She had a particular fondness for snakes. Her autobiography is called *And I'd Do It Again*. When Aimee came through, Rosie lit up from the inside out. Aimee was so full of life, *she glowed*, even filtered through a much more reserved personality.

Rosie loves to travel and was flirting with the idea of retiring. She's especially close to two of her granddaughters and worries about how they'd fare in her absence. Though Rosie's very good at her job in customer service, she is annoyed by some of their ridiculous time-wasting protocols. Rosie was so afraid of taking action when it came to her retirement she devised a way to get her employer to ask her to leave! She simply stopped following some of their silly rules.

During Rosie's QHHT® session, Aimee reminisced about her wonderful adventures, especially in the Far East. She encouraged Rosie to set a retirement date and begin planning. Her granddaughters would not only do well in her absence, they would ultimately flourish due to their free-spirited grandmother's influence.

During Rosie's QHHT® session, we asked Aimee if Rosie agreed to have more fun in her life, would she be willing to stay on as a spirit guide? Aimee agreed. When Rosie walked out of her QHHT® session, Greg was astonished. She looked like a different person. A luminous, more confident Rosie was not only ready to get busy making retirement plans, *now she had Aimee Crocker as her travel agent!*

Rosie met with her leadership team to officially reduce her workload, which had doubled over time. Her employer relaxed some of their protocols, and less than a year after her QHHT®

session, Rosie gave notice that she'd be retiring in early 2024 to tour South America.

One of my more interesting QHHT® sessions was with a Caucasian client I'll call Loretta, who adopted two little girls from China. Several of Loretta's incarnations featured her oldest daughter. Though she loves her madly, Loretta and her daughter have what she describes as a turbulent relationship.

The first life Loretta visited was in China. She was Chinese in this incarnation. She and her husband were minor royalty who lived in a palace. Loretta was a very beautiful woman named Liang. Her husband's name was Chiang. Liang had a traditional upbringing in which she was expected to marry and be subservient to her husband. Loretta's oldest daughter in this lifetime was Liang's oldest daughter in that lifetime. Liang raised her strong-willed daughter to believe in herself and to be independent.

When Liang's daughter grew up and was told by her father that she must marry, she was furious. Her father's edict went against everything her mother had taught her. It wasn't the kind of life she expected to live. The daughter eventually acquiesced. She married and raised a family, but she continued to resent her mother for making her believe she would get to be her own person.

The next lifetime Loretta visited was in Egypt. Loretta was a man whose job was to supervise the building of a pyramid. It required a lot of people and focused concentration to levitate the stones and put them into place. Loretta's oldest daughter in this lifetime was her daughter in that lifetime as well. He considered his life a happy one until his beloved daughter was bitten by a spider. She died at age nine. Though there were other children, she was his favorite. He never got over her loss and consequently ruined his relationship with his wife and sons by virtue of his devotion to his daughter's memory. He was eventually bitten by the same type of spider and died.

The lifetime Loretta chose to visit next was a hundred and fifty years in the future, when she and her oldest daughter would reincarnate together as identical twins. They'll be very close their entire lifetime. The challenge will be to live separate lives as adults with their own husbands and children. They're both neuropsychologists who work with traumatized children. In the future, neuroplasticity of the brain will be used to create new neural pathways. The work is very exciting and rewarding. The twins will work together initially but ultimately decide to live an hour apart for the sake of their families.

Though the lifetime she'll share with her daughter is over a hundred years away, knowing they'll be together again in the future gave Loretta a sense of peace about their current relationship. She could relax and stop trying so hard to win her daughter's affection. The more Loretta backed off, the friendlier her daughter became. They are currently enjoying a less dramatic relationship that satisfies Loretta's need for her daughter's affection and her daughter's need for independence.

Like Hamlet, when I ponder the nature of reality, I believe there's much more out there than we can see, hear, or imagine. As a QHHT® practitioner, I'm more convinced than ever that there are other dimensions, realms, and lifeforms. A client I'll call Eliza visited several lifetimes where her sole purpose was her energetic presence in a specific location. In those lifetimes, she was alone with no husband or children or family of any kind. Though she lived a solitary existence, she was aware of her purpose and never felt lonely. One of those lifetimes was in the twelfth dimension, with many different lifeforms. There is a being like Sasquatch that smells horrible. Eliza is a fairy. There are unicorns and the dragonflies are so large the fairies can ride them.

Eliza experienced two lifetimes as a warrior goddess. In one, her purpose was to teach the children. In another, she lived with the soldiers. It was her responsibility to prepare the men for battle. She practiced a ritual with each of the men that involved bathing in a special kind of water and having sex. Her current husband was one of the soldiers from that lifetime.

The next lifetime we visited was during a prehistoric time. Eliza lived alone with a daughter, who is her daughter in her current lifetime. The only reason they were still alive is she and her daughter weren't present when wild animals killed the rest of their clan, including her mate, who is her current husband. Before Eliza died in that lifetime, her daughter found love and acceptance in a new clan where she had a family of her own.

Several clients have experienced lifetimes as fairies. I showed up in one. When a client, whom I'll call Catherine, arrived that morning, we did her pre-session interview outside. I live on a man-made lake with many plants, gnomes, rocks, and birds. Catherine found it very fairylike. During her QHHT® session, when we asked Catherine's subconscious if we'd known each other in a previous lifetime, she was shown the two of us as fairy sisters. I do indeed feel very fairylike.

So far, I've shown up in one form or another in four of my clients' QHHT® sessions. There is the lifetime as a cellular biologist in Atlantis, the lifetime as a fairy, the lifetime where I attended a séance with Helena Blavatsky, and in a QHHT® session with my niece, Cassie, I was a slave in Louisiana. Cassie was the daughter of the plantation owner. The first words out of her mouth were, *"I'm a rich white woman!"* and she burst into tears.

When I remarked that most rich white women aren't dismayed by their wealth, she added, *"We have slaves! They sold her!"* she said, sobbing.

"Who did they sell?" I asked.

"My best friend!" she wailed.

"How old was she?" I queried.

"The same age as me," she replied, wiping her eyes.

"How old are you?" I asked.

"I'm four," she said, and burst into tears again.

They sold a four-year-old child.

"They sold her," she cried, *"and it's you, Aunt Cindy! She's you!"*

Cassie was able to share a great deal about that lifetime. Her name was Caroline Nantucket, and her father was a plantation owner in Louisiana. She left the plantation for California in her early twenties, where she married an academic named Johnson. They lived in what is now Ione, California, where she worked as a social reform activist in a place of higher learning. When I moved Caroline to an important day in her life, she was jubilant. All her hard work had paid off. "Abraham Lincoln was elected president!" she cried.

In 2017, we recorded the Halloween episode of our YouTube channel, *Chillin' with Adam* from New Orleans, where our special guest, Jim Morrison, performed his last concert. I was dressed as a gypsy. During that episode, I was told I had a previous incarnation in New Orleans where I practiced voodoo. I can't help but wonder whether it was the lifetime with Cassie.

One of my QHHT® clients, Tamara, allowed me to use her real name. Tamara, who no longer identifies as a victim, is determined to heal and actively supports other women doing the same. The lifetime of abuse Tamara described during her QHHT® session was heartbreaking. In a very recent past life, she was a young black woman named Anja in her early twenties who lived in Alabama.

"It's bad," she said.

I suggested she experience it as though she was watching a movie.

Anja was excited about a new job she'd just gotten as an intern at a newspaper. Her abusive husband beat her when he drank. She stayed with him because she had nowhere else to go.

When I moved Anja ahead to an important day, she said, "I'm watching somebody set on fire. Myself. He set me on fire."

I asked if it was the last day of Anja's life.

"Yes," she said.

Anja died at the hands of her abuser at age twenty-four.

"I never got away," she said sadly.

Her life purpose as Anja was to have faith in God. She was shown that lifetime because in this lifetime, Tamara not only got away from her abuser, she's healing from the abuse and helping other women to do the same.

Greg is a strong advocate for women's rights. On Valentine's Day in 2014, he took me to First Presbyterian Church in Oakland, California, to attend an event organized by American playwright Eve Ensler. *One Billion Women Rising* was founded to end rape and sexual violence against women. We arrived at the beautiful and stately old church only to be turned away by a security guard. It was a full house. As a Reiki master and a woman, Greg was certain I was meant to be there. If that was the case, all that was needed is my energetic presence.

I stood in front of the majestic old church with my back against the rail that divides one side of the steps from the other. "Sorry, full house," I listened to the security guard turning people away as I began calling in my support team.

"Jesus, Mary Magdalene, Mother Mary, Archangel Raphael, Archangel Uriel, Archangel Michael, Archangel Metatron, Archangel Gabriel, St. Germaine, Buddha, Quan Yin …"

The moment the steps were filled with ascended masters and avatars, I opened my eyes to see the security guard walking toward me. "You can go in now," he said, adding, "There are two seats on the balcony in the third row against the south wall."

I beamed Reiki to the women who had come to release their anger to make way for healing. These women on their knees were no longer subservient; they came to take their power back. My thanks to Greg for ensuring I was there to support them.

Sometimes we're not victimized by other people but feel victimized by our circumstances. A client I'll call Angela suffers from depression and anxiety because of her trauma-riddled childhood, beginning with her mother's death. She felt as though nothing had ever gone her way. At the time of her QHHT® session, she was one year clean and sober. She and her fiancé were living in a van, and both were attending junior college.

Angela's mother died when Angela was eleven. She was raised

by an aunt who had a good relationship with Angela's younger sister, but she and Angela had always been at odds. Her aunt has custody of Angela's ten-year-old son, and she desperately wants him back.

We visited several important days in Angela's current lifetime. She learned the reason her mother died so young was so she would experience losing the person closest and most important to her, making Angela stronger as a result. We released her anxiety and depression by addressing her anger issues. The day after Angela's QHHT® session, I received a text:

> I feel amazing today! We went on a no cell phone date. I feel like a weight I didn't know was there has lifted. Today I felt at peace for the first time in a while. All day, I kept getting this feeling I can only describe as serenity. Thank you so much for yesterday. I really feel like this is the beginning of an amazing chapter in my life, and you are to thank in more ways than one.

Within a couple of months of her QHHT® session, Angela and her fiancé completed their college semester. He earned a spot on the President's List with a 4.0 GPA. They both got jobs working for a large pet food distributor and share an apartment near their favorite fishing spot. Learning that her mother's death was intended for her benefit changed the lens through which Angela viewed her life. She realizes the best way to honor her mother is by going to court to get her son back and living a joy-filled life.

The most unusual lifetime experienced by a client so far is that of a male client I'll call Armando. Armando, who's in his late thirties, described a lifetime on another planet. When Armando was asked to describe his feet, he said, "There's fog on the ground. Everything's moist and a little cold. My feet aren't human. I have two huge toes and a long heel. My skin is grayish-green. I have long, bony legs with an antlike body in sections. I walk upright. I have several arms with three digits with suction cups on the tips. I'm wearing a type of armor for protection." He experienced life with guarded apprehension.

The air is different from the air on Earth. Though he didn't have a nose, his nostrils were built into his face. He described his head as long and cone shaped. His eyes are large, with two eyelids. He has to blink twice. There are no plants. He doesn't experience hunger.

There are ponds everywhere, but the water isn't normal. They're filled with a thick jelly-like substance that provides them with all the nourishment necessary to sustain life. The slime is gooey but thick enough to hold in his hand. His jaw separates when he puts his face in the pond. He sucks in what he described as live balls that are still moving. He uses his hands to hold on to keep from going in too deep.

He described himself as a type of "fog-being." When the fog lifts, they become terrified. Flying pterodactyl-like beings prey on them. The fog-beings can't see them coming. They live in caves and eat from the ponds. They don't procreate. The planet is outside the Milky Way. Time is different there. There are two suns together. One is red, and the other is a pinkish orange. The fog-beings can only view the sun momentarily when the fog lifts. That's when they're most vulnerable. The fog-beings can jump several stories high. That's how they get around. There is no gravity.

There are thousands of fog-beings like him. The sound they make is like a bubbly clicking and crackling. Speaking is unnecessary. They communicate telepathically, but they can scream to warn others of the pterodactyl-like beings. Anytime one of them screams it's a warning. They know there is danger, and everyone moves. There is safety in numbers. When the fog-beings jump together, it creates the fog that allows them to hide from predators. Predators are afraid of fog-beings in large numbers. In large numbers, the fog-beings can see the light without worry.

While experiencing this lifetime, Armando said he felt a

constant trembling inside. He realized it was the natural state of the fog-being. When the fog-beings are all together as sort of a hive mind, sharing energy, the fog is thick like a blanket. When they vibrate together, it changes the terrain. They're in a constant state of flux. Some die; however, they don't experience sorrow over death.

Their planet is closer to the sun than Earth. It feels good when it's hot, but not when it's cold. The fog-being said, "There's no technology to control the environment."

I found it interesting he would make such a statement. *Does technology control the Earth's environment?*

There are other beings of all colors and shapes that live in caves. They are all able to communicate telepathically. The noises in the pond scare him, so he has to wait to eat. They can only eat when there is light. The goo is alive in the dark, pulling you in, and you get made into goo. The fog-beings are essentially eating the bodies of their dead.

Their planet is so different and so much older than Earth. They must wear equipment to breathe. The fog-beings are hybrids, a product of their genetic mix. Their native species was eradicated by technology. Their mission was to bring balance to the planet so the ponds could get bigger. "We're not allowed to say who put us here," he said, "But we were put here to repair the damage."

The predators control our numbers, so it's a balance. We have a short lifespan. There is no aging. We go willingly to the pond when we feel the calling. It isn't sad as there is no sorrow, only the fear of dying in pieces."

At the end of his life, he went to the pond. It pulled him in like quicksand. There were others with him. They died in groups.

You may wonder how past life regression is relevant to one's current lifetime. During the induction phase of the QHHT® process, the subconscious is directed to go to the most appropriate time and place. We ask the subconscious to scan the body from head to toe and let us know if there are any issues in need of healing.

Some health issues have their basis in a previous lifetime.

Others began with a single symptom to get your attention. The body is quite literal. You get a stomachache when you can't "stomach" something. You get a backache when you're "carrying a heavy load." Unexpressed anger can create liver issues. A lifetime of giving without receiving love in return can cause heart issues.

Sometimes issues are karmic. My losing Adam was part of an agreement to handle grief differently than in a previous lifetime with Greg. Though I suffered many losses in that lifetime, my greatest loss was Greg's untimely death due to a tragic accident.

Greg Adams and I met on e-Harmony in 2006 during his magical birth year, the year he turned fifty-three, the age of the year of his birth. When I met Greg, he was unaware he had heart disease, which is often a silent killer.

My second husband, a psychology professor at a local university, also had heart disease, so I recognized the symptoms. In December 2009, a little over a year before Adam transitioned, Greg had a quadruple bypass, the same surgery, and the same surgeon as the professor. It was as if the universe said, "If you can save him, you can keep him."

Greg often says how lucky he is to have met me when I live in the US, and he's from Canada. Sometimes, I have to remind him that our meeting wasn't just fortuitous; it was preordained. It's one of those immutable events we agreed to before we were born. How would I know him? He would give me back the name I would give my beloved first-born son, the one I would lose in this lifetime.

Chapter 14

Brother Long's Traveling Salvation Show

Any method of evangelism will work if God is in it.
—Leonard Ravenhill

My maternal grandfather was a baptize-'em-in-the-river Pentecostal evangelist. Grandpa was in the business of saving souls. I've come to believe Grandpa had the right idea but the wrong message. His style of preaching encouraged the love of God out of fear of the devil and spending eternity in hell.

I adored my Grandpa Long. Having married at eighteen, he was only thirty-eight when I was born. The year I turned four, when we lived with Grandpa and Grandma Long,

Rev. James Irenus Long, January 25, 1919–September 27, 2000.

he was more like a daddy to me than my own daddy, who worked out of town.

Grandpa bought some land on Highway 67 in Judsonia, Arkansas, where he built a house. Preaching didn't support the family. Grandpa made his living buying and selling used merchandise.

115

There was a good deal of traffic going by, so he added a building that looked more like a warehouse than a secondhand store, but it served the purpose. There were rows and rows of boxes of used merchandise, from tools and toys to kitchenware and clothing.

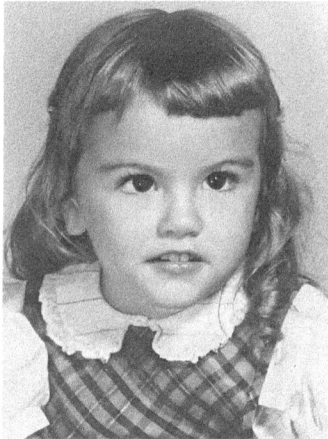

Little Cindy Sunshine makes you happy when skies are gray.

Grandpa rarely left the house without me right on his heels. Speaking in full sentences before I was two, I was cheap entertainment. Grandpa loved telling the story of how, when I was a toddler, I charmed a homely old man at the grocery store into buying me a sack of candy. I assure you, that wasn't my intention. He was the homeliest old man I'd ever seen. He just seemed so sad, I felt compelled to do something to make him feel better.

"You sure are a pretty man today," I said. "Did anyone ever tell you, you're a pretty man?" My eyes were so dark that my penny-pinching Grandpa would offer folks a quarter if they could see my pupils.

Grandpa said the old man had recently lost his wife, and he lit up like a Christmas tree. "Why, that old man bought little ole Cindy a sack of candy as big as she was!" he declared, exaggerating mightily as preachers are prone to doing.

When my daddy was in town, instead of listening to Grandpa preach, I hung out with the men who hung out in the parking lot. I may have been only four, but I took notice when people said one thing and did another or when their description of an event I witnessed with my own two eyes didn't match what actually happened. Hypocrisy 101.

I know too many people calling themselves Christians who profess to respect the religious beliefs of others when what they really mean is that once exposed to *their* religious beliefs if you don't abandon your belief system in favor of theirs, you're going straight to hell.

Some Christians believe that out of the eight billion individuals on the planet, there's only room for 144,00 souls in heaven. Those are the folks doing the most extensive evangelizing. If they truly believe theirs is the one and only true religion, don't they realize all that evangelizing is stacking the odds against themselves?

My grandfather was the seventh of ten children, four boys and six girls. His parents, Willie Dee and Lillie Lee, accused each other of cheating until they finally divorced. I wonder whether Grandpa's passion for religion began as a need for an external sense of control. His newly adopted fear of God curbed his enthusiasm for the worldly pastimes that broke up his parents' marriage.

Grandpa was the youngest person ever to wed in the state of Tennessee. For a short window of time in 1934, it was legal for fifteen-year-olds to marry. Grandpa and his first wife got through the window before somebody came to their senses and slammed it shut. The marriage was over the minute it began. Naturally, they divorced.

Linnie Mae Clark Long,
March 23, 1919–July 18, 1997.

When Grandpa married my grandma, Linnie Mae Clark, in 1937, they were both eighteen. I still don't know how they met. Every time I ask a relative, their memory gets fuzzy, and they mumble something about what a terrible life my grandmother had. Lois, my oldest living aunt, says she thinks they met through Grandpa's brother, John.

Grandma Long was beautiful, especially in her youth; I can only imagine how smitten Grandpa must have been. My mom was born in 1938 when my grandparents were nineteen. Grandpa found Jesus at a revival. He would later testify the night he went down on his knees before Assemblies of God evangelist Rev. Al Ragsdale, "Something got ahold of me."

Grandpa gave up cursing, dancing, betting, and playing cards. As a rule, anything that was formerly fun, besides procreating, was now off-limits. Determined to follow in Rev. Ragsdale's footsteps, he asked Ragsdale to mentor him. Rev. James I. Long was ordained before his second daughter, Lois, was born in 1940.

Grandpa's style of preaching empowered men at the expense of women. Anytime a man strayed, it was the fault of the woman. He'd have remained on the straight and narrow if she hadn't been so tempting.

Mom and Grandpa were never happier than when they squared off across the dinner table, arguing Bible verse. My mother was a feminist, a staunch and loyal supporter of Helen Gurley Brown. After my mom died, I found a copy of Grandpa's last sermon, typewritten on an antique Remington in all caps at age seventy-three after forty-nine years of evangelizing. While Grandpa was in Arkansas painstakingly pecking out his magnum opus, Mom was in California supporting Planned Parenthood and perusing Cosmopolitan magazine. No wonder he and my mom argued.

The following sermon is an appeal to fellow church leaders:

Rev. James I. Long knew how to tune up an audience.

Seeing the pitiful plight of the church, some of the leaders are becoming aware of this condition and want to do something about it, but they seem not to know what's causing the problem and don't seem to know how to take hold of it, or what to do about it. They're getting the cart before the horse and trying to whitewash a fence post instead of replacing it because it's decayed. Let me say, until they are willing to preach hell is hot and eternity is long, they are just spinning their wheels.

God, I pray in Jesus's name that you will take this following message and so burn it in the hearts of preachers and churches that we will begin to see a manifestation of holiness in spirit, worship, prayer, determination, obedience, and dress."

That last part was directed toward women in general. Calling women out was a sure-fire way of stirring up the passion of Grandpa's contemporaries. He implored them to remember the feeling of when they were first saved.

Do you remember when God first saved you? Do you remember how thrilled you were and the great joy, peace, and satisfaction you enjoyed? How you wanted everyone you came into contact with to be saved? You wouldn't dare miss a church night. You had a prayer life, and whenever you had spare time, you grabbed up God's word and couldn't get enough of it.

Your experience was like first love with a sweetheart. When a man falls in love with a woman, he can't do too much for her! He will open the car door for her, and when she steps off the curb, he holds her arm and says, "Oh, honey, watch your step." He can't spend too much time with her and tells folks what a wonderful woman he has found!

When they marry, it's not too long until other things have gotten his attention. He gets home later and if they go to town, she's holding a young 'un and says, "Honey, open the door for me, will you?" and he says, "The door's got a handle, hasn't it?" Whereas before, they were as close as nineteen is to twenty, now she's leading one and carrying the baby. What has happened? He has lost his first love!

It's a shame that there is no more discernment in the churches than today. We have got preachers who are in our pulpits today who are adulterers. They cheat, lie, steal, and walk among us without fear because they know there is not enough discernment to detect them in the churches today! They failed God long ago and don't know any other trade but preaching, and they go on tickling the folks' ears until something bad comes out on them. Well, they couldn't get by with it if the gift of discernment was present!

How sad it is to see some of our church women all painted up like Jezebel or some of the leading figures in Hollywood. I am seventy-three, and when I was a child, people talked against women painting up and felt like only low women did it. Moral, sin-free women had long hair and said only a flapper would cut her hair off, but the women of the night, living the lifestyle they did, didn't have time to fool with long hair, so they chopped it off. How sad to see our church women and even pastors' wives with short hair. They look like a bobbed tail nag. Like a man had messed it up a strand at a time all night in a motel somewhere. Furthermore, it looks like an explosion in a broom factory.

What a shame to see a woman parading around in pants like men wear. Some of the pants are so tight it looks like they were painted on. When they walk away, some of them look like two pigs fighting in a sack. This is an abomination in the eyes of God. We need to preach the fear of God to people until they come crying and crawling on their knees, begging for forgiveness.

Rev. Long knew how to tune up an audience. With each keyword and trigger, they came a little closer to where he wanted them: on their knees.

SONGS
AS SUNG AND PLAYED BY THE
FULL GOSPEL JUNIOR STRING BAND

THIS BOOK FREE TO ALL WHO GIVE AN OFFERING OF 1.00

Long Family Gospel Band,
free to all who give a dollar.

The Long Family Gospel Band was formed when Rev. Long's children were old enough to play stringed instruments. The band featured Rev. Long on the steel guitar, eleven-year-old Lois on the autoharp, ten-year-old Jimmy on the guitar, eight-year-old David on the banjo, and five-year-old Nathan on the mandolin.

When spirits were especially high, the children began switching instruments. Rising to their feet, clapping, stomping, and grinning, the congregation went wild as five-year-old Nathan took over brother David's banjo, blowing an ember to a flame. Once again, the Long Family Gospel Band had set the Lord's house afire with the Holy Spirit.

My thirteen-year-old mother's instrument was her sweet soprano voice, but she preferred singing over the dinner dishes to singing on stage at revivals. The only time she had to herself was when her brothers and sisters were out evangelizing with Grandpa.

The Long Family Gospel Band drew record-breaking attendance across the Bible Belt from New Orleans to Alabama and as far north as Chicago. During Mom's senior year in high school, Rev. Long bought a refurbished bloodmobile, and the Long Family Gospel band prepared to hit the road again.

Refusing to live in a bloodmobile, Mom hopped on the back

of my dad's motorcycle and they headed for Mississippi where they were married on April 13, 1955.

When The Long Family Gospel Band reached Chicago, Grandpa got a job and a basement apartment and decided to stay awhile. Danny, the youngest, was diagnosed with a brain tumor when he was three. The tumor, though not malignant, was considered inoperable. My grandparents were told that even if the tumor were removed, it would grow back.

JUL   55

Long Family Gospel Band with their refurbished blood mobile.

When Danny died in Chicago at the age of eight, I was five and a half months old. My mom, dad, and I were living in Chicago as well. My dad was managing a restaurant. I was only an infant when Danny died, but I never forgot him. My second son, Nathan Joseph, is named after my two youngest uncles, John Nathan and Daniel Joseph. The day Danny died, January 5, 1958, the *Chicago Tribune* sent a reporter to Grandma and Grandpa's apartment.

Danny died on a Sunday just before Grandpa got home from church. Grandpa put Danny's body in the car and drove as fast as he could back to church, where what remained of the congregation prayed fervently over the dead child. When Danny took a breath, it was declared a miracle. Though Uncle Danny only lived for about an hour, it was enough to interest the newspaper.

My grandparents hadn't sought medical treatment for Danny because they'd already been told the tumor was inoperable, but the newspaper jumped at the chance to humiliate Rev. Long into going back to Judsonia. The Long Family Gospel Band stayed in Chicago less than two months after the publication of the newspaper article.

The family was gathered at Grandma and Grandpa's apartment

when the reporter arrived. Mama was seated on the sofa with me on her lap. That reporter must've been terribly uncomfortable, given the nature of the task.

Every time I get to this part of the story, I imagine the scene as though it were a movie. In my mind's eye, a well-turned-out Milo Ventimiglia is the reporter wearing a traditional brown tweed suit and brown fedora. Hat in hand, using the most obvious icebreaker available, the reporter sat across from my mother and me. Leaning forward, he reached out and shook my tiny fist, "Hi."

"Hi!" I replied.

"Hi," he repeated, my tiny fist still in his hand.

"Hi!" I echoed," brown eyes twinkling, enjoying his attention.

"How old is your baby?" he asked, surprised that an infant so small could speak.

"Five and a half months old," answered my equally surprised mother. I'm more intrigued that my first word was spoken to a reporter from the *Chicago Tribune* than the fact it was uttered at five and a half months old.

My Scottish friend, Kerry Kennedy, the intuitive who shared the message from my relative whose name starts with a "J," had a reading with Stewart Pearce, a former director of voice for Shakespeare's Globe Theater in London. In addition to his role as a professional voice coach, Stewart channels twelve of the archangels. Kerry found her reading so helpful that she encouraged me to schedule a reading of my own.

Stewart Pearce is the man who softened Margaret Thatcher's edges. Coaching her to drop from her head space into her heart space created a more compassionate version of Margaret, who was much more appealing to the public. From the last part of 1995 through her death in 1997, Stewart was Princess Diana's voice, presentation, and life coach. (Pearce 2020)[12]

According to his book, *Diana the Voice of Change,* Stewart's role was to enhance Diana's presence in the world, including her charitable work. After her divorce from Prince Charles, Stewart helped Diana claim her sovereignty, creating a stronger version of Diana who was more confident, passionate, and persuasive. She stepped into her newly empowered role with a profusion of personal charisma and greater gravitas. (Pearce 2020)[13]. Languid, lovely, and liberated, Diana was magic in motion.

Stewart coached actor Eddie Redmayne for his role as transgender artist Lili Elbe in *The Danish Girl*. Though he was nominated for Best Actor for his performance, Redmayne now believes a transgender actor should've played the role. Stewart coached Mark Rylance, also a former director of voice for Shakespeare's Globe Theater, for his role as the evildoer Abel, in *Bridge of Spies*. Rylance won the Academy Award for Best Supporting Actor in 2016, a month before my reading with Stewart.

Stewart grew up in Buckingham Palace. His father worked for Prince Philip, frequently traveling abroad with him. A very unusual child, Stewart was a synesthete. *He could see sound.* When Stewart heard voices, he saw color. An angry voice manifested as a violent shade of red. Whining and complaining showed up as dark yellow, while his mother's voice was soothing and comforting, surrounding him in pure white light.

We each have a signature note at our very core that carries our own unique frequency, our very own primordial sound, distinctive, and completely autonomous, like our blood, our fingerprints, and our DNA. It was Princess Diana's wish that when the time was right, Stewart would share the vocal exercises and body techniques, prayers, meditations, affirmations, and empowerment exercises that gave her the confidence to claim her sovereignty. Chapter two of *Diana the Voice of Change* contains the techniques Diana used to center, empower, and liberate her being. (Pearce 2020)[14]

My reading took place the day before Easter in 2016. "You," said Stewart, "will be speaking in flames." Flames destroy the old to make way for the new. When he said I would be vilified by my family, he hit the nail on the head. If it isn't in the Bible, it isn't of God, and Reiki isn't in the Bible.

Following a discussion about shamanism, my sister, Karen, conceded, "I didn't get the God gene." Located on chromosome 10, the alleged God gene is associated with a predisposition toward spiritual or mystical experiences. If there is a God gene, I can't help but wonder whether it's triggered by trauma, such as the loss of a child. Like me, my Grandma Long, who was highly intuitive, became even more so after Uncle Danny died.

I am spiritual but not religious. The difference between religion and spirituality is that spirituality doesn't require a mediator and it doesn't come with a mandatory set of rules. That's not to say I don't live by the same rules, but it's not out of fear of an angry God or fear of spending eternity in hell. I've always been more afraid of the people who are afraid of the devil than of the devil himself.

When Stewart learned of my intention to write a book about Adam's transition and my subsequent spiritual journey, he said, "What you have to say … I feel the truth … I feel the impetus … I feel the integrity … and I feel the passion. I also feel the neo-paradigm nature of what you're bringing forth."

Stewart continued, "The angel that appeared in the church over you and Adam was Gabriel, the divine messenger, to prepare you for Adam's death, which would set into motion a series of events. The first of which is the end of your 3-D existence."

When it comes to consciousness-raising, Adam and I are giving away the cheats. Once I realized how mind-blowing this book will be, I questioned why I was chosen to share such controversial information. That my first word was spoken to a reporter at five and a half months is a noteworthy curiosity, but when paired with Gabriel's appearance over Adam and me in the church before Adam's transition, and Stewart Pearce's prediction that I'd be speaking in flames, I became even more determined to know why I was volunteered for the job.

The next part is like a fairy tale. "You carry within your auric field a seal indicating that an aspect of your soul is a priestess anointed in the House of Khonsu, the God of the Moon." The moon has long been associated with cycles of death and rebirth.

"A very ancient part of your soul is coming forth. It has to do with this amazing transition between life and death. *The Egyptian Book of the Dead* is burning through you."

Also known as *The Book of Coming Forth by Day,* the central message of *The Egyptian Book of the Dead* is about navigating challenges and achieving eternal life.

Everyone's name has a meaning. My name means "moon." Cynthia is an epithet for Artemis, the Greek Goddess of the moon, who was born near Mt. Cynthus on the island of Delos. My mother named me Cynthia "because," she said, "you're like the moon, bright and changeable, yet dark and mysterious."

Stewart continued, "Although you've been very effective in 3-D and you've given of your service lovingly and inspirationally, what you were never able to do is to really live your truth because they didn't want you to. Now, you're living your truth.

You've honored the way the tribe wanted you to function. Now your soul is being called to a different degree of service. That's what Adam's passing was all about. You and Adam are from the same soul group. Adam's passing was about his soul learning very powerful things he would be able to share with humanity, serving as a portal between Divine Mind and you."

Based on my experiences with Adam and Rhonda *after* they died, how could I possibly believe that death is an end? As the caterpillar is to the butterfly, death is not an end; it's a transition from one way of being to another.

"If death were a punctuation mark, it would be a semicolon," said Adam, "not a period. You could think of death as a rest stop between incarnations, but the greatest part of your I AM presence cannot be contained in a human body. Part of you is always here at the rest stop. You're so much more than you ever dreamed of being, limited only by your belief system and your imagination."

If you're afraid to question your beliefs and how you acquired them, then whatever you believe came from somewhere outside yourself rather than as a result of your own spiritual development. If communicating with your higher power requires a third party to get Him on the line, so to speak, you've been misinformed.

Have you heard of a single near-death experience where someone came back and said, "Jesus was busy, so I didn't get to meet God?"

Stewart predicted that besides the book and our blog, I'd have a YouTube channel. I couldn't imagine what I'd be doing on YouTube. Less than a year later, we launched our YouTube channel, *Chillin' with Adam*. According to Adam, so many celebrities on the other side want to come forward now that they know they have a forum. Our first guest was one of Adam's all-time favorite people, Bob Marley.

Between April 2017 and February 2018, we visited with David Bowie, Jimi Hendrix and Barry White, Elvis, Albert Einstein, Joe Cocker and Jim Belushi, Annie Sullivan, Florence Nightingale, Ray Charles, John Lennon, Anne Frank, Wyatt Earp and Doc Holliday, John Wayne, Marilyn Monroe, Robin Williams, Clark Gable, Freddie Mercury, Gene Kelly, Hugh Hefner, Jim Morrison, Janice Joplin, Whitney Houston and daughter Bobbi Kristina, Laura Ingalls Wilder, Lou Gehrig, George Michael, Richard Pryor, Prince, and Princess Diana.

Were Grandpa Long alive today, I wouldn't have to ask what he thinks of the guests on our YouTube channel. *"Demons! Every one of them! You better get baptized, girl. Hell is hot, and eternity is long!"*

Chapter 15

Be the Change

"You humans are truly the heroes," a Being told me. "Those who go to earth are heroes and heroines because you are doing something that no other spiritual beings have the courage to do. You have gone to earth to co-create with God." [15]
—*Saved by the Light*, Dannion Brinkley

The whole is greater than the sum of its parts. If God is the whole, we are some of His parts. According to Neal Donald Walsh's *Conversations with God*, as part of God, *we are creator gods ourselves*. According to the Bible, that's blasphemy. Have you ever wondered why?

Q. How do you control eight billion creator gods?

A. You don't tell them what they really are; then you hide the truth that would prove otherwise. If they figure it out, make their actions punishable by death.

The following is paraphrased from *Conversations with God:*

The Three Levels of Creation

THOUGHTS become things. Before a thing can happen, it is first a THOUGHT. THOUGHTS send creative energy into the Universe.

Each WORD we speak is a THOUGHT expressed; therefore, WORDS create even more energy than THOUGHTS.

ACTIONS are WORDS *in motion*. When we change our WORDS, we change our ACTIONS. We create ourselves anew in every single moment *in partnership* with *God*. (Walsh 1995)[16]

As a co-creator with God, what if you could change the world? *You can!* When even *one* of us raises our vibration, it raises the mean vibration of the entire planet. If all it takes to make a difference is one of us, imagine the power we wield as a group!

Everything is energy, and that's all there is to it. Match the frequency of the reality you want, and you can't help but get that reality. That's not philosophy. *It's physics.*

Like a radio station, we experience the reality of the frequency we're flying. What if we don't like the frequency we're flying? We start by monitoring our thoughts. Based on the Law of Expectancy, whatever we focus on expands. We're human; we're not going to stop having negative thoughts. It's OK to notice a negative thought without entertaining it. Don't analyze, moralize, criticize, or dramatize. *Let it go.*

During his near-death experience in 2006, Adam was greatly disturbed by the potential future he saw ahead for mankind. *We experience the reality of the frequency we're flying.* Love is the most powerful force in the universe. *Love conquers all.* From an alien invasion, deadly virus, or vaccine to World War III, regardless of what imprisons us, *love will set us free.*

The more loving, compassionate, generous, and forgiving our thoughts, the higher our frequency. The higher our frequency, the more love, compassion, generosity, and forgiveness we attract. When it comes to frequency, how do we know where we stand? *Glad you asked!* The chart below is based on the work of David R. Hawkins, MD, PhD.

Frequency in Hz	Level of Spiritual Development	Emotionally I feel	I view life as
700-1,000	Enlightenment	Inexpressible joy	Is
600	Peace	Bliss	Perfect
540	Joy	Serenity	Complete
500	Love	Reverence	Benign
400	Reason	Understanding	Meaningful
350	Acceptance	Forgiveness	Harmonious
310	Willingness	Optimism	Hopeful
250	Neutrality	Trust	Satisfactory
200	Courage	Affirmation	Feasible
175	Pride	Scorn	Demanding
150	Anger	Hate	Antagonistic
125	Desire	Craving	Disappointing
100	Fear	Anxiety	Frightening
75	Grief	Regret	Tragic
50	Apathy	Despair	Hopeless
30	Guilt	Blame	Evil
20	Shame	Humiliation	Miserable

Psychiatrist David R. Hawkins, MD, PhD, saw beyond the limitations of traditional psychiatry. Over twenty years of research into human suffering led him to the creation of a map of human consciousness. From shame (20 Hz) to enlightenment (700–1,000 Hz), each level of human consciousness has its own view of life. (Hawkins 2020)[17]

Have you ever noticed how some people are so positive and full of joy they seem to glow? The human race is transitioning from Homo sapiens to Homo Noeticus, the divine human. As human consciousness rises, our DNA is becoming more crystalline than carbon. The more crystalline our DNA, the more light we hold. Raising the frequency of the planet increases the possibility of more favorable outcomes. Who's to say what could happen when enough of humanity reaches the Christ consciousness (500 Hz)? As children of God, do humans not realize their own divinity?

You don't have to die to ascend to a higher level of consciousness. The doorway to heaven lies within your heart. There are as many pathways to heaven as there are souls seeking its solace. Each pathway, while unique in its characteristics, ultimately leads to peace and unconditional love.

In numerology, the number 6 represents harmony and balance. If 600 Hz is the frequency of perfect bliss and illumination, and 700 Hz is pure consciousness (Hawkins 2020);[18] *what if 666 is a frequency* rather than the number of the Antichrist?

Rather than a single event, what if the Ascension is a conscious transformation process by which we not only raise our own vibration, we participate in raising the vibration of the planet? Once we choose a more heart-centered way of living, compassion prevails over indifference, empathy overcomes anger, and love triumphs over fear.

Approximately 85 percent of the world's population is still below 200 Hz. Levels of consciousness below 200 Hz (courage) acquire their energy at the expense of others. When your primary focus is on survival, others are seen as rivals.

How does it look for the future of mankind if only 15 percent of the world's population calibrates over 200 Hz? (Hawkins 2020)[19] *Glad you asked!*

The scale of power advances logarithmically. According to Hawkins, one individual who calibrates at 300 Hz (willingness/acceptance) *counterbalances* ninety thousand individuals who calibrate below 200 Hz. One individual at 500 Hz (love) *counterbalances* 750,000 individuals below 200 Hz.

Based on that premise, with a population of eight billion people, it would take 10,666.6667 individuals who calibrate at 500 hz to raise the mean vibration of the planet to 200 hz, the frequency of courage. Isn't it interesting that the quotient lighting the way to a future free of fear contains the number 666 on either side of the decimal point?

The power of love is 10^{500}, whereas fear is only 10^{100} power. The difference between a loving thought and a fearful thought is so enormous that even one or two loving thoughts a day *counterbalances* all of our negative thoughts by their *sheer power.* (Hawkins 2020)[20]

Grief calibrates at 75 Hz, the emotion of regret. Those who become stuck in grief are calibrating at the frequency of victimhood. What is the one thing a victim lacks? *Power.* Specifically, the power to change the circumstances that led them into victimhood.

What can we do if we can't change the circumstances? *We can change the way we think about them.* Thanks to Adam, once I redefined death from an ending to a new beginning, I've never experienced grief the same way again. Once I could accept Adam's leaving as something that had been planned before either Adam or I was born, I could accept the death of my sister, my stepdad, and my mother.

I understood when my sister, Rhonda, left, she was given a choice, and she took it. When Jim left in November 2018 at age eighty-two, his blood had stopped absorbing oxygen, and nothing could be done about it. When my mom left in August 2021 at age eighty-three, it was her time. She was suffering. Her health had declined to the point that there was no more joy or comfort left for her. How could I be so selfish as to want her to stay?

Demonstrating the courage and willingness to accept responsibility for our own circumstances places us at 200 Hz, above the powerlessness of victimhood, empowering us to shift to a higher level of consciousness. From consciousness 200 Hz (courage) on up, life becomes more harmonious. *Do you want a happier life? Raise your vibes!*

Once I stopped thinking about what I didn't want and started thinking about what I did want, my life changed completely. "The key is will," says Hawkins, "a constantly repeated act of choice. Persistent willingness is the trigger." (Hawkins 2020)[22] According to Carolyn Ford, fulfilling my purpose on earth is all about will. She pointed out the significance of my maiden name, Williams. Will. I. Am.

Some methods of raising our frequency are affirmations; tapping (a form of acupressure); mantras; yoga; Reiki; breathwork; tai chi or qi gong; aromatherapy; positive self-talk; listening to high-frequency music; *avoiding low-frequency music*; exercising; eating well; and avoiding people, places and things that no longer serve us. (Hawkins 2020)[21]

Hawkins's *Map of Consciousness* outlines the path from where we are to where we want to be. His book, *The Map of Consciousness Explained,* can help us get there. Additional methods of raising our frequency are:

Activity	Calibration
A Course in Miracles Workbook: a course of spiritual study that helps us find the love already present in our lives.	600 Hz, peace
Prayer	525 Hz, love
Meditation (Sound of Om)	740 Hz, enlightenment
The Lord's Prayer	650 Hz, peace
The New Testament (King James)	640 Hz, peace
Smudging (clearing your energy field)	520 Hz, love
Sound Therapy (Solfeggio Frequencies)	Between 174 Hz and 963 Hz
Wholetones™ (frequency based music)	From 396 Hz to 852 Hz, reason to enlightenment
Living by the Golden Rule	400 Hz, reason
Random Acts of Kindness	350 Hz, acceptance
Spending time doing what we love	500 Hz, love
Spending time with people we love	500 Hz, love

In November 2012, I attended Dancing in the Light, a retreat facilitated by Baker Gendron, Adam's first spiritual interpreter. The retreat took place in a three-bedroom house on Highway 89a in Sedona. There was no cable television or cell phone service. We were roughing it!

The intention for the retreat was to release that which no longer serves us, freeing ourselves to manifest the life of our dreams. When it was my turn to share, I said I wanted to retire from my job as a special education program specialist to write a book about Adam's transition and my subsequent spiritual journey.

I'd done my Reiki master training in July 2012 and had been practicing Reiki for about a year and a half. Reiki came in handy during challenging IEP (Individual Education Program) meetings, but I wanted to concentrate on my work as an author and healer full-time. I turned fifty-five that summer, so technically, I was old enough to retire.

"Why can't you retire?" asked Baker.

"Financially, it just wouldn't be possible," I said. "I've only been with the school district for sixteen years."

"Can't they make you some kind of deal?" Baker queried.

Once I stopped laughing, I said, "Baker, there are over *three thousand employees* in my school district. I'm nothing special. Why would they offer *me* a deal?"

"I don't know," she replied. "It just came to mind."

In November 2012, retirement felt so utterly impossible that I hadn't bothered trying to manifest a different outcome. I was still spending a lot of time thinking about things I no longer wanted rather than imagining my ideal life *as though it already is.*

Baker paired those of us interested in giving and receiving Reiki with a partner. My partner was Diana, a statuesque blue-eyed blonde in her forties. For a retired military officer, I was particularly impressed by her calm and gentle demeanor. Diana and I took turns clearing each other's chakras or energy centers. The chakra system regulates the flow of consciousness and energy moving within and without our bodies.

When it was my turn on the Reiki table, Diana used a pendulum to measure the activity of each chakra. When she moved the pendulum from my heart chakra to my solar plexus chakra, it hung lifeless. Not so much as a quiver. According to Diana, my willpower was missing in action.

Diana asked me to close my eyes and imagine my ideal life. In my mind's eye, I was retired, spending my time reading and writing and enjoying every minute of my newfound freedom.

"Open your eyes and look at this pendulum," said Diana, the biggest grin on her face. "If this thing swings any higher, it's going to flip right over!"

Once I understood the process, I became a master manifestor. When it comes to the Law of Attraction, the universe doesn't know the difference between what you want and what you don't want, *it matches the pictures in your head*. Things began falling into place once I dialed into my desire for financial freedom and independence.

Two months later, in January 2013, my school district offered a golden handshake to the Pupil Personnel Services union, with the caveat that at least eight members must retire to make it worthwhile for the school district. Determined to find seven other PPS members in search of freedom, I campaigned like a politician the day before the election. In June 2013, seven of my colleagues and I retired!

Fast forward to May 2022, nine years later. Greg and I were at the New Living Expo in San Mateo, California, on Mother's Day. We were registered to hear cellular biologist Bruce Lipton's talk that evening. I got the time confused, and we arrived just as it ended.

My copy of his bestseller, *The Biology of Belief,* in hand, I went to the book signing area. I could say hello and have him sign my book. Bruce Lipton was nowhere in sight.

I went to the room where Bruce had given his talk, and there he was, signing autographs, a line of folks waiting their turn. I got in line with my copy of *The Biology of Belief*. When it was my turn, I told Bruce, "You were expected in the book signing area about half an hour ago. Come with me; you can sign mine when we get there."

Bruce allowed me to escort him to the signing table. There I was, strolling the red-carpet side by side with a bestselling author *on Mother's Day!* When I held my copy of *The Biology of Belief* as high as I could reach, it elicited a giggle from Bruce. There we were, Cindyana Jones and the Pied Piper of Belief Change, headed together to a book signing.

When we reached the author's table, I sat Bruce down on one side and took my place at the head of the line on the other. He reached for my book.

> For Cindy,
> With wishes this science will empower your life!
> Love and Light,
> Bruce Lipton
> May 2022

"Cindy!" he cried with the biggest grin on his face as he handed back my book. Greg captured Bruce's enthusiastic greeting on video. It was so cute I couldn't resist turning the one-second video clip into a meme.

"Cindy!" "Cindy!" "Cindy!" What encouragement! I could watch it all day long. What a fabulous Mother's Day present! *Thank you, Adam!*

Bruce Lipton and me at the New Living Expo, *"Cindy!"*

On Friday evening, the weekend of the New Living Expo, I was sitting up in bed by myself. Adam came in and allowed me to experience what it would feel like to read my book. *It was thrilling!*

He continued showing me passages in the book and how it will feel to read them, then the book turned into a movie, and I got to watch *Adam's Gift* from the audience's perspective.

"This is better than *Steel Magnolias*!" I blurted, relegating my favorite movie of all time to second place.

"We're going to win Best Picture!" said Adam, "Now, go and write the book the movie is based on."

What happened next is right up there with what happened with Johnnie in Mount Shasta in terms of incredulity. A screen appeared between me and the bedroom wall on the other side of the room. I could see the wall through it.

An invisible purple marker began drawing in the air. First, it drew the head of a pig. Then it gave the pig an oval-shaped body, four legs, and a tail. When it drew a wing on the side furthest from me, I was intrigued. I felt like a game show contestant. The instant it added the wing on the side closest to me, I watched in fascination as the pig flew right through my bedroom door! *"When pigs fly!"* I cried.

Will *Adam's Gift* be an Academy Award-winning movie? I have no idea, but who am I to question a prophecy punctuated with a flying pig?

I walked by a tarot card reader at the New Living Expo.

"Would you like a reading?" asked Grandmaster Gerhardt.

"I don't want a reading for myself, but I'd like to know the impact of the book I'm writing, *Adam's Gift*."

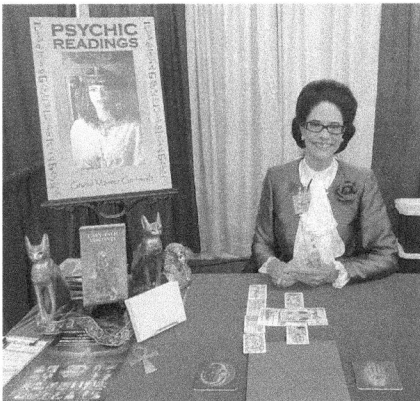

Tarot Card reading for *Adam's Gift* with Grandmaster Gerhardt.

Pulling a card, she said, "The impact of *Adam's Gift* is the chariot card. In terms of effectiveness on your readers, *this* is *the highest-frequency card in the deck!* The Chariot card symbolizes complete victory and moving forward."

She continued, "This is in tune with the mystery school teachings and the overcoming of the lower frequencies from the subconscious. Your readers will be more connected to the hierophant in the future, which represents their higher self. Your book will assist them in changing to a new frequency."

"The Temperance card, which is creating the future from the past, is in the *blocked* position. Your readers will not be doing the same thing they used to do after reading your book. Once they are operating more from their higher self, they will be operating from a position of self-empowerment."

Drop the spiritual mike!

The possibilities are endless! We're not victims of circumstance, fate, or our genes. If we're victims of anything, it's our self-imposed limitations. Our beliefs determine our biology, not the other way around. In *The Biology of Belief,* Bruce Lipton described the life-changing moment when he realized our genes do not control our cells; they're controlled by their *environment.* Who determines our physical and energetic environment? *We do!*

"I was exhilarated by the new realization that I could change the character of my life by changing my beliefs," said Lipton. "I was instantly energized because I realized that there was a science-based path that would take me from my job as a perennial "victim" to my new job as co-creator of my destiny." It is not gene-directed hormones and neurotransmitters that control our bodies and our minds; our *beliefs* control our bodies and our minds and, therefore, our lives. (Lipton 2016)[23]

When I met Bruce Lipton, he was seventy-seven years old and every bit as happy, vital, energized, and engaged as he was when he authored *The Biology of Belief.* He chose happiness, and he continues to choose happiness every day.

Formerly a self-described card-carrying rationalist, Bruce said he's come full circle. We're not powerless biochemical machines. We are made in the image of God. When we want to improve our spiritual and mental health, we must put *spirit* back into the equation. (Lipton 2016)[24]

New research has consistently validated Bruce's skepticism

about the primacy of DNA controlling life. Epigenetics, the study of the molecular mechanisms by which the environment controls gene activity, is one of the most active areas of scientific research today. (Lipton 2016)[25] We may inherit a predisposition for something that can be managed by controlling the environmental factors that trigger those genes.

Our subconscious mind controls 95 percent of our behavior. You'd be surprised at how many self-imposed limitations come from within. How did they get there? From the moment we're born, the adults around us begin shaping our belief systems based on their own. We pass our faulty belief systems down from one generation to the next. What if we could ferret out those faulty beliefs and reprogram them? *We can!*

A variety of exciting techniques can be used to access and reprogram beliefs that no longer serve us. QHHT® (Quantum Healing Hypnosis Technique), developed by Dolores Cannon, works directly with the subconscious. A technique called Psych-K® combines psychology, kinesiology, neurolinguistic programming, and whole-brain integration to identify and change long-standing limiting beliefs in minutes. Psych-K® is the easiest, quickest, and safest way of reprogramming the subconscious. Psych-K® originator, Rob Williams describes Psych-K® as a spiritual process with psychological benefits.

Bruce Lipton witnessed Rob's work at a conference where they were both presenters. Rob asked the audience if anyone would like to address an issue that had been troubling them. When a woman in the audience timidly raised her hand and spoke her fear aloud, she spoke so softly that Rob had to take her aside to learn that her greatest fear was speaking in public.

He worked with the woman for about ten minutes using a Psych-K® technique. "The change was astonishing," said Bruce. After one session with Rob, the woman took over the stage while the audience sat with their mouths agape, eyes like saucers. (Lipton 2016)[26]

Few things are as rewarding as empowering others to take charge of their lives. As a QHHT® practitioner, I've witnessed the unparalleled healing power of the subconscious. With Psych-K®, we can rewrite our own software by identifying and reprogramming the subconscious beliefs that are holding us back.

After listening to Bruce Lipton's life-changing testimony on YouTube, I researched Psych-K®. I was so impressed with Psych-K®'s efficacy as a stand-alone healing modality and the perfect complement to QHHT,® that I became a certified Psych-K® facilitator. Unlike QHHT,® which must be done in person, Psych-K® sessions can be facilitated online or over the phone.

BQH, (Beyond Quantum Healing), developed by Candace Craw-Goldman, a student of Dolores Cannon, is similar to QHHT®. The primary focus of BQH is to facilitate healing, gain insight, and enhance spiritual growth. BQH sessions can be facilitated remotely. I'm thrilled to be working with such powerful, life-changing techniques. The possibilities are unlimited.

Nothing unburdens our hearts like forgiveness. One of the simplest, most powerful tools I've encountered is the *Ho'oponopono,* a traditional Hawaiian practice of reconciliation and forgiveness. The process allows us to rid ourselves of emotional burdens that prevent us from healing.

The first step is to say, *"I'm sorry,"* accepting responsibility for what you intend to heal, regardless of whether it's a situation, an illness, or a relationship.

Step two is asking for forgiveness. Say, *"Please forgive me,"* as you remember your remorse from step one.

Step three is showing gratitude. *"Thank you."* Thank you to yourself, to your higher power, or to a former nemesis for accepting your forgiveness.

Step four is saying *"I love you"* to yourself, to your higher power, and to those you have forgiven.

If we're all part of God, we're all part of each other. I would be remiss if I didn't share how the *Ho'oponopono* was used to cure an entire ward of criminally insane patients. From 1983 to 1987, Dr. Ihaleakala Hew Len, a psychiatrist at Hawaii State Hospital, reviewed each mental patient's file; then, *without ever meeting a patient face-to-face,* he used the *Ho'oponopono* to heal the part of himself he shared with them. Within four years, all the patients had been released and the ward was closed.

Just as fish are surrounded by the ocean, humanity is surrounded by Source or God energy —a field of infinite absolute radiant potential. Set your intention to consciously evolve moment by moment, one day at a time, by staying in the present moment and taking responsibility for your thoughts, words, and actions. *Focus your attention on your intention.* Where your attention goes, energy flows. Match the frequency of what you desire, and you can't help but receive it. It can be no other way.

One of the oldest battles in the history of mankind is the inner tug of war between love and fear. *While fear holds us prisoner, love sets us free.* Love doesn't seek to vanquish the enemy. Love seeks a way to coexist despite our differences. If, in every situation, we choose love, *we will create the world we wish to see.*

Say it with me: "I choose to create a world of compassion and a future free of fear. I choose *love.*"

Epilogue

A Conversation with Adam

"Adam, I'm still having a hard time getting my head around the intergalactic part of the story. I've had the least amount of direct experience in that area." Adam grins like he knows something I don't.

"You *remember* the least amount of experience in that area. Mom, what you can't remember would fill a whole library."

"Maybe because it still feels a little bit scary here in 3-D," I said. "My primary concern is accuracy. I want to be sure what I'm reporting is as factual as possible."

"Would the US have a space force if there was no threat to Earth's safety?" he reasoned.

"People are still struggling to think globally," I said, "and we're asking them to think intergalactically. How important is it that we share the intergalactic piece?"

"It's very important because it's real," said Adam, "and it's paramount to life and understanding."

"Are you still with the Galactic Federation?" I asked.

"Yes," answered my multidimensional, multitalented, multitasking son.

"But you incarnated here as Adam..." Before I could finish the sentence, Adam interjected, "On a temporary basis."

"Was it always intended that you would leave before your twenty-eighth birthday? I asked.

"Yep," said Adam. "I reached my expiration date."

"Then you would share information back through me to keep your promise to God and your country?" I asked.

"Yes," said Adam. "You and I had a special bond. You furthered the bond when you made it a priority to understand what happened to me and our life together. I was given the latitude to do many things on Earth, but it wasn't easy to adapt once I got there."

I needed to know. "When you wrote your poem about flying away when that light shines, were you referring to being picked up by the Galactic Federation?"

"Yes," he replied. "I knew that would happen when it was my time."

"You *knew* they would pick you up?" I asked, wondering how Adam managed to keep all that to himself. Or did he? Thinking back to that day in my kitchen, "One of these days, I'm going to fly away in the delta," and the poem I found after Adam's transition, *Fly Away*.

I know now when it's my time, once that light shines, I'm gon' fly far away.

That's as close as he got to telling me while on this side of the veil. "Yes," he admitted. He knew.

"So, your consciousness went aboard the ship and merged with an aspect of you who was already there?" I clarified.

"Yes," said Adam.

"In terms of your body, do you look like a human?" I asked. Trying to imagine my son as a being of another species, I added, "Do you look like a Zeta or a Mantid?"

"I can present myself in many different aspects," said Adam, "but I look more human than anything else."

"What is your role with the Galactic Federation," I asked. "What do you do?"

"We're part of a group that does rescue missions," said Adam. "Then we ensure the beings we protect are on a sustainable path. We're not required to exterminate any individuals or beings of any race. Evil is not just on Earth; yet fighting evil doesn't work either.

"Earth has complicated the situation because not enough

people are on the same page. People on earth believe they're more special than they are. When they feel threatened, they've still got that intimidation thing going on because that's how they control the world.

"That's unacceptable," he added. "It's not our job to force people to do anything. The regulation of Earth is a disappointing thing for all of us, yet we carry on."

"Is our book going to help?" I asked.

"Love and understanding — the energy in our book — is what the earth needs now," he said. "Our book will initiate conversations that lead to understanding. It's a little on the lame side and simplistic, but nobody cares enough about everybody else."

Concerned for the future of the planet, I queried, "Will Earth finally be accepted into the Galactic Federation?"

"They will," assured Adam. "They're closer than they imagine. Going to Earth was a memorable experience. I'm so happy it was with you because I'm still with you."

My heart swells as I feel the connection with my son that began before he was born. I shudder as I realize I could have ignored that connection out of ignorance; or allowed it to become overshadowed by grief when Adam transitioned thirteen years ago.

"I'm so glad you're still with me too," I said, blinking away tears. I still miss Adam's physical presence. I'm human.

"What will it take to create peace on Earth? I asked.

"Remember that Coke commercial where everybody is holding hands?" said my son, now an intergalactic guardian.

"I'd like to teach the world to sing in perfect harmony?" I sang.

"That's the one!" said Adam. "Let's add a line."

As I closed my eyes and imagined everyone on the planet holding hands, Adam invoked the following words, "Let there be peace on Earth, and let it begin with me."

And so it is!

Notes

Introduction

1 Neale Donald Walsh, *Conversations with God, Book Three*. (Hodder & Stroughton Ltd, 1998), 58.

2 Dannion Brinkley, *Saved by the Light*. (Vallard Books, 1994), 29–49.

Chapter 2

3 Gary E Schwartz, PhD, and William L. Simon, *The Afterlife Experiments: Breakthrough Scientific Evidence of Life After Death*. (Atria Books, 2002), 254, 257.

Chapter 4

4 Sherrie Dillard, *I'm Still with You: Communicate, Heal & Evolve with Your Loved One on the Other Side*. (Llewellyn Publications, 2020), 120.

5 Barbra Streisand, *My Name is Barbra*. (Viking, 2023), 513-515.

Chapter 8

6 Cindy Williams Adams. *"Adam's 11th Anniversary Gift: $108.00 Jackpot on a Penny Slot Machine."* Adam's Gift (blog). July 10, 2018. https://www.adamsgift.net/adams-11th-anniversary-gift-108-00-jackpot-on-a-penny-slot-machine/.

Chapter 12

7 David Blaine, "Harrison Ford Finds Card in Orange: Real or Magic/ David Blaine," January 8, 2014. Video. https://youtu.be/rB0wzy-xbwM.

8 Chillin with Adam, *"Chillin' with Adam with David Bowie #2,"* April 10, 2017. Video, 31:33. https://youtu.be/T2KUybklBF4?t=1893.

9 Cindy Williams Adams. *"Chillin' with Adam with Elvis, The King of Rock & Roll, Mama and Baby Bro!"* Adam's Gift (blog). May 2, 2017.

https://www.adamsgift.net/chillin-with-adam-with-elvis-the-king-of-rock-roll-mama-baby-bro/.

10 Dropout, *"Fart Spelling Bee,"* November 17, 2009. Video. https://www.youtube.com/watch?v=arXMhMJbT0U.

11 Chillin with Adam, *"Cindyana Jones & The Adam Skull with Carolyn Ford & Einstein,"* April 14, 2024. Video. https://youtu.be/5WHMrGBCyGU.

Chapter 14

12 Stewart Pearce, "Diana the Voice of Change." (Shimran, 1998), 1.

13 Stewart Pearce, "Diana the Voice of Change." (Shimran, 1998), 12.

14 Stewart Pearce, "Diana the Voice of Change." (Shimran, 1998), 66, 106.

Chapter 15

15 Dannion Brinkley, "Saved by the Light." (Vallard Books, 1994), 45.

16 Neale Donald Walsh, *"Conversations with God, Book One."* (Hodder & Stroughton Ltd, 1998), 164.

17 David R. Hawkins, MD., PhD, *"The Map of Consciousness Explained."* (Hay House, 2020), 51.

18 David R. Hawkins, MD., PhD, *"The Map of Consciousness Explained."* (Hay House, 2020), 81, 82.

19 David R. Hawkins, MD., PhD, *"The Map of Consciousness Explained."* (Hay House, 2020), 38, 117.

20 David R. Hawkins, MD., PhD, *"The Map of Consciousness Explained."* (Hay House, 2020), 63, 118–119.

21 David R. Hawkins, MD., PhD, *"The Map of Consciousness Explained."* (Hay House, 2020), 329–331.

22 David R. Hawkins, MD., PhD, *"The Map of Consciousness Explained."* (Hay House, 2020), 278.

23 Bruce H. Lipton, PhD., *"The Biology of Belief."* (Hay House, 2016), xv.

24 Bruce H. Lipton, PhD., *"The Biology of Belief."* (Hay House, 2016), xxvi.

25 Bruce H. Lipton, PhD., *"The Biology of Belief."* (Hay House, 2016), xxiv.

26 Bruce H. Lipton, PhD., *"The Biology of Belief."* (Hay House, 2016), 230-232.

27 Psych-K® Free your Mind, *"Bruce Lipton shares how Psych-K® Changed his Life,"* February 12, 2022. Video. https://youtu.be/WT61BpFxtkg.

Book Club Questions and Conversation Starters

Did reading Adam's Gift prompt you to explore your own spirituality and beliefs regarding life after death? If so, how?

Have you ever received signs from a loved one or a spirit guide on the Other Side? If so, what kind of signs did you receive?

Did you embrace the communication or try to talk yourself out of believing it?

Did you tell anyone? If so, did they believe you? How did that feel?

Were there any specific stories or symbolism in the book that resonated with you?

Which chapter of Adam's Gift was your favorite and why?

How did the author explore spirituality?

If you could ask the author one question, what would it be?

What is your overall impression of Adam and what gift did you receive from reading our story?

Do you believe humans are the only intelligent lifeform in the universe?

Do you believe disclosure will occur in our lifetime?

Do you believe that fear is a choice and we have the sovereignty to choose how we feel?

What puts you into fear and what can you do to change how you feel?

Do you believe you have the power to identify and change beliefs that no longer serve you?

As children of God, do you believe we have the ability to ascend to a higher level of consciousness *before we die?*

What is your dearest wish and what can you do to see it come to fruition in your lifetime?

Would you like to go on a wild goose chase with Adam? Just ask him, then don't forget to follow the clues. Email us at cin@ adamsgift.net and tell us all about it.

101 Spiritually Influential Books

A Course in Miracles, Text, Workbook for Students, Manual for Teachers, Helen Shucman, PhD

A Hypnotist's Journey from the Trail to the Star People, Sarah Breskman Cosme

A Hypnotist's Journey to Atlantis: Eye Witness Accounts of our Ancient History, Sarah Breskman Cosme

A Hypnotist's Journey to the Secrets of the Sphinx, Sarah Breskman Cosme

A New Earth, Eckhart Tolle

A Return to Love: Reflections on the Principles of A Course in Miracles, Marianne Williamson

Amazing Grace: The Nine Principles of Living in Natural Magic, David Wolfe

Anatomy of the Spirit: The Seven Stages of Power and Healing, Caroline Myss

Ask and it is Given: Learning to Manifest Your Desires, Esther Hicks

Autobiography of a Yogi, Paramahansa Yogananda

Awakening to the Spirit World, Sandra Ingerman and Hank Wesselman

Becoming Supernatural: How Common People are Doing the Uncommon, Dr. Joe Dispenza

Beyond Positive Thinking: A No Nonsense Formula for Getting the Results You Want, Dr. Robert Anthony

Bringers of the Dawn, Barbara Marciniak

Buddhism: Beginner's Guide to Understanding and Practicing Buddhism to Become Stress and Anxiety Free, Michael Williams

Change Your Thoughts, Change Your Life: Living Wisdom of the Tao, Dr. Wayne Dyer

Conversations with God (Books One through Three), Neale Donald Walsh

Creative Visualization, Shakti Gawain

Destiny of Souls, Michael Newton

Dying to be Me, Anita Moorjani

Evidence of Eternity: Communicating with Spirits for Proof of the Afterlife, Mark Anthony

Good Vibes, Good Life: How Self-Love is the Key to Unlocking Your Greatness, Vex King

Hands of Light: A Guide to Healing Through the Human Energy Field, Barbara Brennan

Holy Bible: 21st Century King James Version, KJ21 Bible Publishing

How to Talk to the Dead in 10 Easy Steps, Rhys Wynn Davies

Infinite Possibilities: The Art of Living Your Dreams, Mike Dooley

I'm Still With You: Communicate, Heal & Evolve with your Loved One on the Other Side, Sherrie Dillard

It Didn't Start with You: How Inherited Family Trauma Shapes Who We Are and How to End the Cycle, Mark Wolynn

Journey of Souls: Case Studies of Life Between Lives, 5th Revised Edition, Michael Newton

Life After Life: The Bestselling Original Investigation That Revealed "Near Death Experiences," Raymond A. Moody, Jr., MD

Limitless Mind: A Guide to Remote Viewing and Transformation of Consciousness, Russell Targ

Llewelyn's Complete Book of Chakras: Your Definitive Source of Energy Center Knowledge for Health, Happiness, and Spiritual Evolution, Cyndi Dale

Loving What Is, Revised Edition: Four Questions That Can Change Your Life, Byron Katie

Many Lives, Many Masters: The True Story of a Prominent Psychiatrist, His Young Patient, and the Past Life Therapy That Changed Both Their Lives, Brian L. Weiss, MD

My Son and the Afterlife, Elisa Medhus, MD

Never Letting Go: Heal Grief with Help from the Other Side, Mark Anthony

Noetics: The Science of Reaching Man's Highest Potential, Ramesh Nathan

Oneness, Ratha

Peace is Every Step: The Path of Mindfulness, Thích Nhất Hạnh

Proof of Heaven: A Neurosurgeon's Journey into the Afterlife, Eben Alexander, MD

Real Magic: Ancient Wisdom, Modern Science, and a Guide to the Secret Power of the Universe, Dean Radin, MD

Resilience from the Heart: The Power to Thrive in Life's Extremes, Gregg Braden

Return to Life: Extraordinary Cases of Children Who Remember Past Lives, Jim B. Tucker, MD

Saved by the Light: The True Story of a Man Who Died Twice and the Profound Revelations He Received, Dannion Brinkley

Seth Speaks, Jane Roberts

Signs: The Secret Language of the Universe, Laura Lynn Jackson

Spirits Beside Us: Gain Healing and Comfort from Loved Ones in the Afterlife, Chris Lippincott

The Afterdeath Journal of an American Philosopher, The View of William James, Jane Roberts

The Afterlife Experiments: Breakthrough Scientific Evidence of Life After Death, Gary E. Schwartz

The Afterlife Frequency: Scientific Proof of Spiritual Contact and How That Awareness Will Change Your Life, Mark Anthony

The Afterlife of Billy Fingers: How My Bad-Boy Brother Proved to Me There's Life After Death, Annie Kagan

The Artist's Way, Julia Cameron

The Awakened Family: How to Raise Empowered, Resilient, and Conscious Children, Shefali Tsabary, PhD

The Bhagavad Gita, Vyasa

The Biology of Belief: Unleashing the Power of Consciousness, Matter & Miracles, Bruce Lipton, PhD

The Body Keeps the Score: Brain, Mind, and Body in the Healing of Trauma, Bessel van der Kolk, MD

The Book of Awakening: Having the Life You Want by Being Present to the Life You Have, Mark Nepo

The Book of Joy: Lasting Happiness in a Changing World, Dalai Lama and Desmond Tutu

The Book of Knowledge: The Keys of Enoch, J.J. Hurtak

The Celestine Prophecy, James Redfield

The Children of Now, Dr. Meg Blackburn Losey

The Choice: Embrace the Possible, Dr. Edith Eva Eger

The Divine Matrix: Bridging Time, Space, Miracles, and Belief, Gregg Braden

The Emotion Code: How to Release Your Trapped Emotions for Abundant Health Love, and Happiness, Dr. Bradley Nelson

The Empowered Empath: A Simple Guide on Setting Boundaries, Controlling Your Emotions and Making Life Easier, Judy Dyer

The Field: The Quest for the Secret Force of the Universe, Lynne McTaggart

The Four Agreements: A Practical Guide to Personal Freedom, Don Miguel Ruiz

The Gnostic Gospels, Elaine Pagels

The HeartMath Solution: The Institute of HeartMath's Revolutionary Program for Engaging the Power of the Heart's Intelligence, Doc Childre

The Heart of the Buddha's Teaching, Thích Nhất Hạnh

The Highly Sensitive: How to Find Peace, Develop Your Gifts, and Thrive, Judy Dyer

The Holographic Universe, Michael Talbot

The Honeymoon Effect: The Science of Creating Heaven on Earth, Bruce Lipton, PhD

The Light Between Us: Stories from Heaven. Lessons for the Living., Laura Lynn Jackson

The Miracle of Mindfulness: An Introduction to the Practice of Meditation, Thích Nhất Hạnh

The Nature of Personal Reality: Specific, Practical Techniques for Solving Everyday Problems and Enriching the Life You Know, Jane Roberts

The Power of Intention, Dr. Wayne W. Dyer

The Power of Now, Eckhart Tolle

The Science of Mind, The Complete Edition, Ernest Holmes

The Seat of the Soul: The 25ᵗʰ Anniversary Edition with a Study Guide, Gary Zukov

The Secret, Rhonda Byrne

The Secret Life of Plants, Peter Tompkins

The Seth Material, Jane Roberts

The Seven Spiritual Laws of Success: A Practical Guide to the Fulfillment of Your Dreams, Deepak Chopra

The Source Field Investigations: The Hidden Science and Lost Civilizations Behind the 2012 Prophesies, David Wilcock

The Tapping Solution: A Revolutionary System for Stress Free Living, Nick Ortner

The Universe Has Your Back: Transform Fear to Faith, Gabrielle Bernstein

The Untethered Soul: The Journey Beyond Yourself, Michael A. Singer

The Voice of Knowledge: A Practical Guide to Inner Peace, Don Miguel Ruiz

The Way of the Peaceful Warrior: A Book That Changes Lives, Dan Millman

The Wisdom of Frances Scovel Shinn, Frances Scovel Shinn

Think Like a Monk: Train Your Mind for Wisdom and Purpose Every Day, Jay Shetty

Three Waves of Volunteers, Dolores Cannon

Touching the Light: Healing Body, Mind, and Spirit by Merging with God Consciousness, Dr. Meg Blackburn Losey

Transforming Anger: The HeartMath Solution for Letting Go of Rage, Frustration, and Irritation, Doc Childre

Urban Shaman: A Handbook for Personal and Planetary Transformation Based on the Hawaiian Way of the Adventurer, Serge Kahili King, PhD

When Things Fall Apart: Heart Advice for Difficult Times, Pema Chodron

You Can Heal Your Life, Louise Hay

You'll See It When You Believe It: The Way to Your Personal Transformation, Wayne W. Dyer *Zen*

Zen Mind, Beginner's Mind, Shunryu Suzuki

Milton Keynes UK
Ingram Content Group UK Ltd.
UKHW011028240624
444593UK00010B/134/J

9 781665 757805